SCHOLAR Study Guide

SQA CfE Higher Business Management Unit 3: Management of People and Finance

Authored by:
Julie Sanderson (West Calder High School)
Alan Hamilton (Stirling High School)

Reviewed by:
Frances McCrudden (The Mary Erskine School)

Previously authored by:
Alistair Wylie
Rhona Sivewright
John Murray
Peter Hagan

Heriot-Watt University
Edinburgh EH14 4AS, United Kingdom.

First published 2015 by Heriot-Watt University.

This edition published in 2015 by Heriot-Watt University SCHOLAR.

Copyright © 2015 SCHOLAR Forum.

Distributed by the SCHOLAR Forum.

SCHOLAR Study Guide Unit 3: SQA CfE Higher Business Management

1. SQA CfE Higher Business Management Course Code: C710 76

ISBN 978-1-909633-36-0

Print Production and fulfilment in UK by Print Trail www.printtrail.com

Acknowledgements

Thanks are due to the members of Heriot-Watt University's SCHOLAR team who planned and created these materials, and to the many colleagues who reviewed the content.

We would like to acknowledge the assistance of the education authorities, colleges, teachers and students who contributed to the SCHOLAR programme and who evaluated these materials.

Grateful acknowledgement is made for permission to use the following material in the SCHOLAR programme:

The Scottish Qualifications Authority for permission to use Past Papers assessments.

The Scottish Government for financial support.

The content of this Study Guide is aligned to the Scottish Qualifications Authority (SQA) curriculum.

Contents

Topic 1

Recruitment and selection

Contents

Learning objectives

After studying this topic, you should be able to:

- *describing methods used to ensure there are effective human resources available;*

- *compare internal and external methods of recruitment;*

- *describe elements of workforce planning;*

- *identify and describe methods of testing;*

- *explain the benefits of flexible working.*

1.1   Workforce planning

Successful businesses must ensure the needs of their customers are always met by finding the right people at the right time with the right skills. They do this to ensure the business is always well staffed with highly qualified employees who work to achieve the business' goals. In today's competitive environment, where profit and bottom line is everything, businesses must ensure that levels of staffing are appropriate; too few staff and the business' reputation will suffer, but too many staff and the business will fail to be competitive. Workforce planning is the term used to describe forecasting future supply and demand to ensure an organisation is always appropriately staffed.

The first stage in this process is to carry out a labour market analysis. This can be completed by the organisation or a third party business (outsourced). It looks to see who is available in the market and if they labour available have the skills the business is looking for.

In addition, a business will look to previous years to determine staffing for seasonal changes. A decision has to be made regarding the hiring of new external staff or if planning internal changes would better suit the business' needs.

A business must think more flexibly if it is to keep up with workforce changes: the notion of a person having the one job for life is no longer accepted. As the needs of individuals have changed, organisations have had to adapt. An increase in part-time working has led to more women seeking work. Woman have been starting families later in life, opting to path out a successful career first to ensure financial stability before planning for a birth. Government legislation has changed drastically over the years, with the addition of equal rights for female workers. Changes in technology allow for work to be completed remotely and the ageing population has seen a need for people to adapt.

Businesses are much more likely to hire seasonal or fixed term staff to cover busy periods. It is common for such a worker to have many different jobs over the course of a year. Whilst this pattern brings challenges to businesses, in terms of continuity of service and induction training costs, benefits can also be seen, as today's workforce is better skilled and prepared to adapt.

These benefits include a workforce that is more responsive to change, reduced costs for a business as more employees chose to work from home, greater motivation and performance as employees are able to focus better on their employment and fit the needs of work around the needs of family.

Flexible working patterns

Q1: Match the working patterns bellow with the following specifications.

Go online

1. Part-time working
2. Flexi-time
3. Job-sharing
4. Home working
5. Teleworking
6. Term-time working
7. Staggered hours
8. Shift-working

a) Working from your car or other remote locations.

b) Widespread in industries, which must run on a 24-hour cycle, such as newspaper production, utilities and hospital and emergency services.

c) An employee may only work 2 or 3 days per week instead of the traditional 5.

d) New technology makes communication with office and customers possible by telephone, fax and email from home.

e) Employees may be required to work within essential periods but outside 'core times' they often get flexibility in how they work their hours.

f) Employees in the same workplace have different start, finish and break times - often as a way of covering longer opening hours.

g) Typically, two employees share the work normally done by one employee.

h) An employee on a permanent contract takes paid or unpaid leave during school holidays.

. . . .

1.2 Job analysis

Businesses need to take a holistic look at their workforce to determine where and when a vacancy may exist. They need to take account of future demand and the existing skillset of the workforce. A business will look to see if any areas of the business are overstaffed and if moving staff within the business may be possible. Writing a job analysis is the first step in the recruitment process.

To complete a job analysis a business would have to look at what are the job's main features.

It will include:

- the main physical and mental elements of the job;
- the specific skills that are required;
- who the job holder would be responsible for;

- who they would be responsible to;
- the location where they will work;
- the main health and safety considerations.

This provides the basis for the job description.

1.3 Job description

Once the job analysis has been completed, and a vacancy identified, the next step is draw up a description for the job. This could be used as the basis for an advertisement of the vacancy as it will let any applicants decide if they want the job.

The organisation needs to think through what tasks they want the post holder to perform.

It will include:

- the job title;
- the overall purpose of the job;
- the main tasks and responsibilities;
- what decision-making powers they have;
- who they are responsible for and to, and who they will work with;
- the skills, qualifications, and experience required to do the job;
- where the job will be based;
- the resources required to do the job;
- conditions of service such as details of pay and conditions available to the post holder; hours of work, and holiday entitlement.

Q2: Outline two reasons for drawing up a job description.

. . . .

Q3: List some details covered in a job description.

. . . .

1.4 Person specification

The main purpose of the person specification is to identify the individual that you want to do the job.

The HR department should identify:

- what physical attributes the successful candidate should have in respect of personal appearance, etc.;
- what skills, educational qualifications, training and experience the candidate should have;
- what level of intelligence is needed;
- what kind of personality is preferred;
- what special skills are required.

This will be used to match against job applicants so it is easier to identify who you want to interview.

Once the job analysis and description have been completed the organisation must decide how they are going to recruit the member of staff.

The first decision is whether to recruit internally or externally.

Recruitment process - descriptions

Fill each blank space with one from the following terms.

Go online

- job analysis
- job description
- person specification

Q4: The purpose of a _____ is to find out whether a vacancy exists and what the job will be.

....

Q5: The purpose of a _____ is to identify what tasks the organisation wants the post holder to perform.

....

Q6: The purpose of a _____ is to identify the individual that you want to do the job.

....

1.5   Types of recruitment

Internal recruitment

Internal vacancies are usually advertised within the business. Existing employees find out about vacancies by looking at staff notice boards or on the organisations intranet. Emails and staff meetings can also be used to let people know about internal vacancies.

Some vacancies can be offered on a secondment basis. This would be useful when a short-term vacancy is required. An individual on secondment temporarily works in a different department. A fixed time will be agreed between the existing department and the seconded department. A new fixed term contract will be issued and there will be no break in the employee's service to the business. This is a good way to ensure continuity whilst ensuring workforce planning.

A suitable candidate may already work for the organisation, so they could simply promote someone within the organisation.

There are several advantages in recruiting internally.

- The costs involved in promoting internally are lower than recruiting externally.

- Advertising the post in newspapers etc, selecting from a wide range of applicants, and the cost of induction training can be avoided.

- The person is already known to the organisation and so the risk of appointing the wrong person is reduced.

- The existing employee will have benefited from the organisation's own investment in training and so this will not be lost if the employee has to leave in order to get promotion.

- The prospect of internal promotion can be a strong motivator for employees, and helps in external recruitment where promotion possibilities are available.

Large organisations will use internal recruitment as they have a large pool of workers that they can pick from.

There are also several disadvantages in only using internal recruitment.

- It restricts the number of applicants for the post as the best person for the job, in the long run, may not yet work for the organisation.

- New workers can bring new skills and ideas to the organisation.

- Promotion will probably create another vacancy which will then have to be filled.

External recruitment

There are a variety of different methods for recruiting staff from outside the organisation. Which is used depends on the nature of the post involved.

For example, if you wish to recruit unskilled or semi-skilled labour you could use the local Job Centre, or advertise in a local newspaper.

If the post is a temporary one you could use a local employment agency. For example, local health trusts use nursing agencies to fill short term shortages in ward staff.

For management posts you could use national newspapers that will have set days each week for recruitment. This has the benefit of attracting the widest range of interested applicants with the right qualifications for the post.

For specialist staff, such as software designers, there are trade magazines that are read by most of these specialists, or you could use a specialist 'head-hunting' agency that will have lists of specialists for a range of areas.

There are also many businesses specialising in Internet recruitment. They attract a range of applicants for either specific jobs or for jobs the applicants would like which will be available in the future. They match their database of applicants with jobs. Recruitment websites allow prospective employees to enter their details and set up email alters. This way, new vacancies that match their skills set are sent directly to their inbox.

Social media also has an active role in the external recruitment process. Many businesses advertise and recruit for new talent through their Facebook and Twitter pages. Social networking site LinkedIn provides users with an opportunity to create a profile showcasing their previous experience and skills. Other users in the form of colleagues and clients can endorse them to raise their profile. Businesses can use this site to vet potential employees.

There are several advantages in recruiting externally.

- There is a larger pool of potential employees.
- It brings new ideas in with the new employees.
- The applicants from out with the firm may bring with them new experiences which may prove useful to the firm.

There are also several disadvantages in using external recruitment.

- It can take a long time to attract someone from out with the firm.
- It can be more expensive than recruiting internally as you have to advertise and go through interviews which takes time and money.
- It is difficult to really know a person having just met them at an interview therefore selection process may not lead you to the best candidate.

Sources of recruitment

Go online

For each question categorise the following terms as **internal** or **external** sources of recruitment:

Q7: Word of mouth

....

Q8: Recruitment drives

....

Q9: Intranet

....

Q10: Head-hunters

....

Q11: Job centre

....

Q12: Trade journals

....

Q13: Noticeboards

....

Q14: Internet

....

Q15: Email

....

Q16: Staff newsletters

....

1.6   Selection methods

When selecting the most suitable candidate there is a sequence of steps that should be involved. The first is to find out if the advertising process has been successful. Have you attracted the sort of candidates you were looking for? If not then re-advertisement may be necessary.

Application forms

The most common form of notification of interest in the position is the application form, however, some organisations still prefer to have applicants submit a Curriculum Vitae (CV), whilst for some vacancies a simple telephone call may be all that is required.

- Application forms are popular because they give applicants the same questions and opportunities to describe themselves.

- It is easier to compare information from a large number of candidates.

- The application forms will be compared to the person specification to see which appear to match.

- The HR department will then look at all the applications and decide which applicants to reject at this stage.

- All rejected applicants should be sent a letter advising them that they have been unsuccessful.

- From the applications that appear to be suitable, a decision must be made as to how many should be invited for interview.

- The number to interview depends on the organisation, however, interviews represent a cost to the business and this should be kept as low as possible.

- The organisation will need to balance this with having a good selection of candidates to choose from.

- Applicants under consideration should be invited for interview, and references sought from existing or previous employers or schools.

Q17: Applications forms are used because:

a) it makes it easy for applicants to complete.
b) applicants have to hand write their answers.
c) all applicants answer the same questions.

....

Q18: The application forms will be compared to:

a) the person specification.
b) the job analysis.
c) the job description.

....

Q19: Which of the following is the correct procedure when recruiting new staff?

a) All applicants should be invited for an interview.
b) The most suitable candidates will be sent a letter of rejection.
c) The most suitable applicants will be invited for interview.

....

Q20: The job advert should be based on:

a) the job analysis.
b) the application form.
c) the job description.

....

Q21: A successful advert will:

a) attract lots of candidates some of whom will be unsuitable.
b) attract a number of suitable candidates.
c) attract few applications.

....

1.7 The interview

Interviews are the most common form of making a final decision on which applicant will be employed. This will be based on who is the best match to the person specification.

It should also be remembered that the interview is a 2-way process. It is an opportunity for the applicant to find out more about the job and the organisation. It may be that at the end of the interview process the applicant decides that the job is not for them.

Successful interviews happen when:

- the interviewer(s) have prepared fully for the interview, with set questions, with full information on what is required;
- it may be helpful to prepare a checklist in advance;
- they also require training in interview techniques which will allow the interviewer to compare candidates more equally;
- the interviewers are not persuaded by the appearance, personality and the interview techniques of the applicant;
- they bring the best out of each candidate, by being open-minded and unbiased towards candidates, making them welcome and relaxed, control the interview, and ensure that all relevant information is gained and given.

Interviews do help in the selection process in identifying the personality and characteristics of the applicant, and also gives some indication of how they react in stressful situations.

References

These are used to confirm that the person who is applying for the job is who they say they are. They are normally written statements from previous employers or other reliable person who can give information about the applicant to the potential employer, stating, for example, whether they are suitable for the post, how reliable they are.

References should be open and unbiased.

1.8 Testing

Aptitude test

These tests measure how good the applicant is at a particular skill such as mathematical skills, typing or shorthand speeds, driving ability, etc. These tests are objective in that each applicants performance can be measured and compared.

You must remember that people perform differently under test conditions than they would in their normal working day and this should be taken account of. This can be done through giving the candidate a number of opportunities to perform at their best.

Psychometric tests

These tests are designed to measure the personality, attitudes and character of the applicant. They are timed tests, usually multiple choice, taken under exam conditions and are designed to measure the intellectual capability of the applicant for thinking and reasoning, particularly logical/analytical reasoning abilities.

They are designed to be challenging but should not depend on having prior knowledge or experience of the post applied for.

Psychometric testing is most commonly used in management and graduate recruitment. However, doubts have been expressed as to how accurate and valid these test are. If the questions are not prepared properly they will give an unfair advantage to certain types of applicant and should be checked for social, sex or racial bias.

Personality tests

A personality test is a set of questions intended to find out about a prospective employee's personality traits so that the employer can make better judgements about whom to hire.

These can give an indication as to whether they are a team player or not, and what team role or roles they perform best. For example, Belbin's self-perception inventory is commonly used by organisations to establish how the applicant will fit into an existing team.

Types of selection methods

Q22: Match the selection method in the first list with the most appropriate description in the second list.

Go online

1. Aptitude test
2. Job description
3. Reference
4. Interview
5. Psychometric test
6. Application

a) A list of what tasks they want the post holder to perform.
b) A two-way conversation between the organisation and the applicant.
c) A questionnaire supplied by the organisation to be completed by the applicant.
d) Designed to measure the personality, attitudes and character of the applicant.
e) A written statement from previous employers or other reliable person.
f) A measure of how good the client is at a particular skill.

. . . .

1.9 Summary questions

Go online

Summary questions

Q23: Most people today will have one job for life.

a) True
b) False

....

Q24: More woman seeking work has led to an increase in part-time working.

a) True
b) False

....

Q25: Term-time workers do not work during school holidays.

a) True
b) False

....

Q26: Teleworking involves holding meetings using the television.

a) True
b) False

....

Q27: Writing a person specification is the first stage in the recruitment process.

a) True
b) False

....

Q28: The purpose of a person specification is to identify the individual that you want to do the job.

a) True
b) False

....

Q29: An individual on secondment temporarily works in a different department.

a) True
b) False

....

Q30: Head hunters are a good example of an internal source of recruitment.

a) True
b) False

....

Q31: Most businesses will ask for both a completed application form and CV.

a) True
b) False

....

Q32: An aptitude test shows a candidates competency in a certain skills, such as driving or language.

a) True
b) False

....

1.10   End of topic tests

End of topic 1 test

Q33: Match the terms (1-10) with the appropriate definitions (a-j).

Go online

1. Application form
2. Aptitude test
3. Home working
4. Job analysis
5. Job description

6. Job sharing
7. Person specification
8. Psychometric tests
9. Teleworking
10. Workforce planning

a) New technology makes communication with office and customers possible by telephone, fax and email from home.
b) Two employees share the work normally done by one employee.
c) An assessment, usually completed online, designed to show the personality, attitudes and character of the applicant.
d) A series of questions on a form.
e) A document outlining the skills, qualities and experience needed of the individual seeking employment.
f) A document outlining the purpose of the job and the hours to be worked.
g) Ensuring you have the right people, with the right skills, at the right time.
h) A brief document outlining a vacancy that requires to be filled.
i) Working from your car or other remote locations.
j) An assessment designed to show how competent a candidate is in a certain skill, such as driving.

....

Q34:

Reorder following sentences (a-l) into the correct order (1-12) of the recruitment and selection process.

a) Advertise either internally or externally, making use of the information contained in the job description and person specification.

b) Inform the successful candidate and invite them to sign a contract of employment.

c) Carry out a labour market analysis to see if there will be staff available when needed.

d) Receive application forms or CVs.

e) Complete a job description highlighting the requirements of the job, including length of contract and the duties of the prospective candidate.

f) Inform all other candidates that they have been unsuccessful. Offer feedback on their application.

g) Carry out a job analysis to see if a vacancy exists.

h) Invite candidates to interview.

i) Conduct one-to-one, panel or group interviews.

j) Complete a person specification looking at the experience, skills and qualifications of the prospective candidate.

k) Review application forms and references.

l) Carry out an assessment centre activity or a series of tests.

. . . .

SQA style questions

Go online

Q35: Discuss the use of external sources of recruitment. (9 Marks)

. . . .

Q36: Outline flexible working practices that an organisation could use. (11 Marks)

. . . .

Q37: Discuss the use of external sources of recruitment. (5 Marks)

. . . .

Topic 2

Training and development

Contents

Learning objectives

After studying this topic, you should be able to:

- *describe methods used to ensure staff are appropriately trained;*

- *describe the objectives of professional development through staff training schemes;*

- *discuss the relevance of training to an organisation;*

- *evaluate the different methods of training;*

- *identify and describe costs and benefits of virtual learning facilities and work-based qualifications.*

2.1 Methods of staff training

Successful training will help update the skills of the workforce and therefore improve employee satisfaction.

Employees represent one of the most important resources of the organisation, so the introduction of a staff training and development programme will assist the organisation to get the best possible return from its investment in the workforce.

The other important fact to remember is that it will improve the image of the organisation. Organisations which offer good training will find it easier to attract new staff, be more likely to attract business, and may qualify for quality awards.

Because of this training should be a continuous process for successful organisations.

Induction training

This is for new members of staff. Its purpose is to:

- make them more aware of what is expected in the tasks they are expected to perform;
- allow them to quickly develop an awareness of the organisation's policy and practices;
- allow them to become familiar with their surroundings.

This will include simple things like where the toilets, break rooms and fire exists are, and much more complicated issues such as Health and Safety policy. It will depend on the type of organisation but it could also include the correct use of equipment; machinery training or the need for protective clothing.

Depending on the job and the organisation, the induction training may take a day or a matter of weeks to complete. All new employees should receive induction training prior to beginning their employment.

Induction training is only effective if it is carried out successfully. Too often it is not given the required time or commitment from management. Induction training is expensive to organise - a cost that has to be repeated if a new employee leaves as a result of ineffective training.

On-the-job training

This takes place while the employee is actually doing their job. It can take a number of forms:

- a more experienced employee showing another worker how to do a job;
- the more experienced employee may watch and offer advice and instruction while the other worker completes the task (coaching);
- the employee may work in different departments or areas of the organisation learning what each does.

On the job training provides both the employee and the trainer the chance to learn new skills but it can also be challenging as both employees may be expected to complete their work at the same time. Internal trainers may not have all of the necessary skills to pass on to the trainee and bad habits can easily be picked up.

Off-the-job training

Off-the-job training is any training that takes place when the employee is not carrying out their usual duties. It can take place in a training room in the office or factory, or externally at a designated training providers workshop or hotel. The organisation may have its own Training Department where it organises its own courses, or it may invite in specialists to train staff.

The employee may be sent to training courses organised by trade associations or employers associations, or to obtain qualifications from college or university. The use virtual, or e-learning, is becoming a popular choice for an employer engaged in off-the-job training.

2.2   Work based training

In an effort to cut costs and improve efficiency, many UK organisations are introducing their own work-based training schemes. Companies such as PricewaterhouseCoopers, KPMG, British Airways, Network Rail, Vodafone, Unilever, Siemens and John Lewis have created their own training schemes that allow employees the chance to gain academic qualifications whilst on the job . Youth apprenticeships and graduate training programs are examples of work based training. Employees can complete their work-based training scheme on an ongoing, daily basis, whilst completing their normal duties (on-the-job training) or whilst away from their normal routine (off-the-job training). Most will involve a mixture of the two.

2.3   Virtual learning facilities

The use of e-learning has increased dramatically in recent years. This is down to the necessity for cost saving exercises as well as improvements in, and access to, technology. Much early experience was based on the use of web-based modules accessed at an individual's computer. In reality, as a learning tool, e-learning is much broader.

There are 3 types of e-learning:

- **Formal e-learning:**
  Technology is used primarily to deliver formal content (such as training or development courses) to the employee without significant interaction with (or support from) training or learning professionals, peers or managers. (Companies such as PriceWaterCoopers).
  http://www.telegraph.co.uk/education/universityeducation/10699245/Company-tr aining-schemes-biggest-threat-to-universities.html

- **Informal e-learning:**

Beyond the formal or 'course-based' approaches to e-learning are the growing opportunities for technology to support informal learning in the workplace. Access to online communities or social media such as Twitter and LinkedIn has led to a growing number of professionals creating informal, but meaningful, professional dialogue communities online.

- **Blended or supported e-learning:**
  Formal and/or informal e-learning may be combined (or 'blended') with other types of learning.   For example, the majority of learning content may be delivered through face-to-face lectures or coaching and/or through textual material, but the dialogue with other learners, the conduct of collaborative activities and the searching for/access to supporting material are all conducted online.

Find out more

1. **Open university**

   Access the Open University and spend 20 minutes looking through a course that interested you. Pay attention to the layout, amount of material and use of questioning.

   http://www.open.edu/openlearn/about-openlearn/try

   Stuck for a topic idea?

   Try http://www.open.edu/openlearn/education/essay-and-report-writing-skills/content-section-0
   This will help you when come to plan and write your CfE Higher Business Management assignment.

2. **Research internet**

   Use the keywords 'twitter professional learning communities' and read 3 useful webpages. Summarise your findings in a short report (250 words). Include your 3 sources in your report. Use the title "Social Media as a method of staff development".

   Show your teacher your finished report. Even better, share your report on twitter using **#SCHOLARBM** and interact with other learners currently studying CfE Higher Business Management.

(You may find this guide helpful:
https://support.twitter.com/articles/215585-getting-started-with-twitter)

. . . .

2.4   Objectives of professional development

There are four major objectives in staff training and development:

- The first is to allow all workers to achieve the level of performance of the most experienced workers. For new workers this would be included in their induction training.

- The second is to make a wide pool of skills available to the organisation both for now and for the future.

- The third is to develop a knowledgeable and committed workforce, which will be highly motivated.

- Lastly, to ensure that the organisation can deliver high quality goods or services.

Organisations have an obligation to develop their staff. By developing a programme of professional development organisations:

- encourage staff to reach their potential;

- increase productivity and output;

- lower staff turnover;

- attract higher quality candidates.

Professional development can be conducted by the organisations staff, outside training providers, online training providers or completed by the individual concerned.

2.4.1 Benefits and costs of training

It is important to let all staff know that they are valued and appreciated. Various methods of performance appraisal can be used and an important output from this process should be an assessment of an employee's training needs. Training programmes should be focused on meeting those needs.

Benefits of effective training:

- Employees feel more loyal to the business.

- Shows that the business is taking an interest in its workers.

- Employees should benefit from better promotion opportunities.

- Employees will be more productive, benefiting the organisations.

- Employees feel more confident in carrying out activities and when dealing with customers.

- Less waste, in terms of spoilage and lost time.

Costs:

- Sending staff on courses will involve a number of financial costs including travel and subsistence.
- It also means that they will be away from their jobs, leaving the organisation with a choice of accepting lower output, or bringing in other staff to cover.
- Whilst training the quality and quantity of their output could reduce.
- If the organisation has its own training department, then staff here will add additional employment costs to the business.
- Once qualified, staff may leave for better paid jobs. On the other hand, some staff may not want the training.

The costs of not training

- Additional recruitment costs when new skills are required.
- Untrained staff are less productive or motivated; accidents are more frequent.
- Workers who are not in a process of training and development are far less likely to be aware of the organisation's objectives.

Costs of training

Go online

Q1: Complete the paragraph using following words.

replacement	additional	quantity
training	job	trained
money	away	quality

While they are away training, the _____ and _____ of employees work can fall. _____ employees may be able to get a better _____ elsewhere. The staff in the _____ department will be an _____ cost for the business. _____ staff will have to be brought in while staff are _____ raining. Training will cost the business _____ .

. . . .

2.5 Summary questions

Summary questions

Q2: Training should be seen as a continuous process.

a) True
b) False

Go online

....

Q3: "Off-the-job" training can involve attending an external training course.

a) True
b) False

....

Q4: "On-the-job" training involves being coached by a college lecturer.

a) True
b) False

....

Q5: Training helps reduce staff turnover.

a) True
b) False

....

Q6: Induction training takes place once per year.

a) True
b) False

....

2.6   End of topic tests

Revise this topic before trying the end of topic tests.

Go online

End of topic 2 test

Q7:   Match the type of training (1-5) with the appropriate definition (a-e).

1. Induction training
2. "On-the-job" training
3. "Off-the-job" training
4. Work based training
5. E-learning

a) Training that takes place instead of the employee completing their work, at the employees work or at a training provider.
b) Training that takes place online using either a training provider or professional learning communities on social media.
c) Basic training for new employees.
d) A long term approach where an employee is trained by the organisation.
e) Training that takes places whilst the employee is working.

. . . .

Q8:   Complete the paragraph using following words.

e-learning	turnover	external	development	internal
"on-the-job"	induction	"off-the-job"	productivity	

_____ training is for new members of staff. Its purpose is to give new staff members the best possible start. A business that is fully committed to staff _____ will give employees a variety of training options. This is because they see the value in developing staff, both to increase _____ and efficiency, whilst reducing staff _____. _____ training takes place whilst the employee is completing their daily routine. It usually involves being coached or mentored by a colleague. Conversely, _____ training takes place when the employee is not involved in their usual routine. This may take place during a training day organised and managed by the business, or at an event being promoted by an _____ training provider. To save costs and improve efficiency, many large organisations have abandoned the more traditional training providers and are creating their own _____ work based training schemes. Many others are taking to the Internet to provide _____ opportunities for staff.

. . . .

Go online

SQA style questions

Q9:   Describe types of training used by a large business. (5 Marks)

. . . .

Q10:   Justify the use of staff training for an organisation. (4 Marks)

. . . .

Topic 3

Motivation and leadership

Contents

Learning objectives

After studying this topic, you should be able to:

- *describe theories of motivation;*

- *describe approaches used to motivate staff;*

- *describe leadership styles;*

- *describe advantages and disadvantages of employee participation;*

- *describe the role of management in motivating employees.*

3.1   Motivation

It is important that a business understands what motivates its employees. A motivated workforce will strive to do better, produce more, work faster and achieve goals. Many research based theories exist to suggest how and why workers need to be motivated.

3.2   Abraham Maslow

Maslow was an American researcher who put forward a theory of motivation in 1954. He suggested that all worker's needs are complex, but that they can be classified into 5 categories. Each category works in a hierarchy, ranging from lower to higher, and that each lower need has to be satisfied before the higher need can be achieved.

Maslow believed that physiological needs are basic, such as food, clothing, shelter and warmth. This can be extended to ample breaks and a good salary to allow a worker to pay for essentials such as food and mortgage repayments.

The second is security or safety needs which can be satisfied through various employment laws, the security of a trade union membership or a contract of employment giving worker rights.

The third is social needs which can be satisfied with a feeling of acceptance and belonging to a team. In the workplace, this can mean belonging to a team or social clubs. Job rotation, where two employees switch jobs to learn new skills, allows both employees to gain new skills and experiences.

The fourth, self-esteem needs, recognise achievements and the need to be appreciated. This can be satisfied through promotion or the receiving of a job title.

The final is self-actualisation. This need can be satisfied through meaningful work assignments where the employee can demonstrate innovation and creativity. Self-actualisation talks of self-fulfilment - the setting of own goals and then the progress an employee makes towards achieving them. Setting, and achieving, the goal of becoming self-employed, for example.

Hierarchy of needs

Q1:

Place Maslow's five factors in the correct order.

Go online

- Social
- Physiological
- Esteem
- Self - actualisation
- Safety

1. _____
2. _____
3. _____
4. _____
5. _____

Hierarchy of needs - definitions

For each question categorise one of the following five Maslow's factor.

Go online

1. Social
2. Esteem
3. Self - actualisation
4. Physiological
5. Safety

Q2: Making the employee feel valued and recognising their job title and place within the business.

Q3: Offering permanent contracts to encourage the feeling of security.

Q4: The basic needs that the employee will satisfy through the receiving wages.

Q5: Allowing the employee to make their own independent decisions and goals.

Q6: Encouraging team work and job rotation; allowing employees to learn from and encourage one another.

3.3 Douglas McGregor

McGregor proposed in 1960 that there are 2 approaches to motivation - Theory X and Theory Y. He did not believe that managers should look at employees as being one or the other, as both were extremes, but that employees could show traits of both.

Theory X (Authoritarian)

If you believe in this theory, you believe that people:

- naturally dislike work and will try to get out of it if they can;
- have to be threatened with punishment and supervised to get tasks done;
- want to be told exactly what they have to do;
- have security as their greatest need.

Theory Y (Democratic)

If you believe in this theory, you think that people:

- think work is fulfilling and natural;
- are able to use self-discipline to achieve their objectives;
- want to be given responsibility and decision making powers;
- have self-actualisation as their greatest need.

Go online

Douglas McGregor - Theory X and Theory Y

Q7:

Use the following statements to complete the table.

1. "I have a sense of pride in my work and everything I have achieved."
2. "Money is the only thing that matters to me."
3. "I enjoy my work as I am given praise when I do well."
4. "If I want extra responsibility my boss will find a way to give it to me."
5. "I'm content where I am."
6. "I don't want promotion, who can be bothered with the hassle?"

Theory x	Theory Y

. . . .

3.4 Frederick Herzberg

Frederick Herzberg published his findings on motivation in 1959, in his book The Motivation to Work. In his publication, he states that there are 2 factors of motivation: motivators and hygiene factors.

Herzberg's research proved that people will strive to achieve these 'hygiene' needs because they are unhappy without them, but once satisfied the effect soon wears off - that satisfaction is temporary. He believed that people are only truly motivated by enabling them to reach for and satisfy the factors that Herzberg identified as real motivators, such as achievement, advancement and development represent a far deeper level of meaning and fulfilment.

Examples of Herzberg's 'hygiene' needs (or maintenance factors) in the workplace are:

- the relationship between a manager and subordinate;
- working conditions;
- salary;
- company car;
- status within the organisation;
- job security.

Herzberg's research identified that 'true motivators' were other completely different factors, namely:

- achievement;
- recognition;
- work itself;
- responsibility;
- advancement.

Essentially, Herzberg said that hygiene factors were important but short lived and that motivators were the things that drove workers to improve. He also believed that employees who demonstrated increasing levels of ability should be given increasing levels of responsibility and that if a job cannot be designed to use an employee's full ability then that job should be automated or the worker replaced with one with a lower skill level. His work was often criticised as he only studied skilled workers. However, many of his findings are still used today as non-financial motivators.

Frederick Herzberg - Hygiene factors and motivators

Q8:

Go online   Use the following factors to complete the table.

1. Recognition
2. Good wages
3. Company benefits
4. A love of the job
5. Supervisors
6. Challenging work
7. Sense of achievement
8. Company policies

Hygiene factors	Motivators

. . . .

3.5 Approaches used to motivate staff

Many approaches are used to motivate staff. The approach used will depend on the organisation and the culture of the managers and employees. If you believe in Hertzberg's hygiene factors then you will have a clear career structure to provide opportunities for promotion. Employees who are motivated by money will work harder to increase their chance of securing the promotion.

Organisations must also ensure they offer good pay and conditions to keep employees satisfied. They should carry out staff appraisals where employees meet with their line manager to discuss their progress within the business. This ensures employees are listened to, meeting Maslow's fourth level Esteem needs.

An alternative is to offer permanent contracts so employees feel they have job security. Successive Governments have promised to end the use of 'zero hour contracts' where employees do not know what hours they will be earning one week to the other. This lack of job security is often a huge de-motivator.

Other financial rewards can be offered. Schemes such as Performance Related Pay, where employees receive bonuses or additional payments for doing a good job or meeting targets, are becoming popular.

Job rotation is a non-financial reward, where employees are regularly moved teams. This allows the employee to gain new skills and experiences that help when going for promotion or new opportunities.

All of this leads to a more motivated workforce. Motivated employees are likely to be more productive and more efficient, meaning the business benefits from a greater quality and quantity of output. Businesses in the service sector benefit from having staff who have a better relationship with customers, leading to a better service and consumer spend.

3.6 Leadership styles

Douglas McGregor, when describing managers as 'theory X' or 'theory Y' was describing leadership styles. He believed that 'theory X' managers where autocratic leaders - they make decisions without consulting others. Autocratic leaders do not listen to others; they dictate rules and policies and do not allow employees to discover ideas for themselves. As a result, employees can be demotivated and feel stifled.

Democratic leaders include team members in the decision-making process. They encourage creativity, and people are often highly engaged in projects and decisions. As a result, team members tend to have high job satisfaction and high productivity. Democratic leaders encourage employees to reach their potential by setting their own agenda. A downside of democracy is that quick decisions cannot often be made as too many people are involved in the process.

Laissez-faire leaders give their team members a lot of freedom in how they do their work, and how they set their deadlines. They provide support with resources and advice if needed, but otherwise they don't get involved. This autonomy can lead to high job satisfaction, but it can be damaging if team members don't manage their time well, or if they don't have the knowledge, skills, or self-motivation to do their work effectively. Laissez-faire leadership can also occur when ineffective managers don't have control over their work and their people.

Hertzberg wrote that employees who demonstrated increasing levels of ability must be given increased responsibility. Businesses must recognise that the ability to empower an employee to self-motivate will result in increased employee participation.

Works councils

Works councils are groups of employees who are given time out of their normal work routine to meet to discuss decisions made by the business. They have the right to request information from management. Since 2000, European legislation has ruled that any business with more than 1000 employees must make provision for a works council to be set up.

Works councils allow employees to have a say in how the business is run. Members feel empowered as they are being listened to. However, businesses do not need to act on the suggestions of the works council, which may be demotivating to the members of the council. Organisations also risk a fine if they do not set up a council after being asked to do so. Not all employees can join the works council which may lead to arguments as to who is in the best position to join. Members of the council may be putting their own needs ahead of others, which could lead to further disagreement.

Worker director

This is when an employee is invited onto the Board to ensure workers have an input into the decision making process. The worker sits on the board to express the views of all employees, not necessarily his or her own views. In the UK, there is no requirement for an organisation to invite a worker to sit on the board. Regular meetings with trade union delegates is a more common way for management to gauge the views of the workforce.

Consultative committees

Employee participation involves management actively encouraging staff to assist in running and improving business processes and operations. At various times, committees may be set up to seek the views of certain employees. These committees are on-binding, meaning the business does not have to act on the advice put forward by employees.

3.7   Summary questions

Go online

Summary questions

Q9:   Maslow described 6 factors in his hierarchy of need: Physiological, safety, social, emotional, esteem and self-actualisation.

a) True
b) False

. . . .

Q10: McGregor believes you either naturally dislike work or think work is fulfilling and natural.

a) True
b) False

. . . .

Q11: Mayo's findings talk in terms of motivators and hygiene factors.

a) True
b) False

. . . .

Q12: Maslow believes that one need must be met before a worker will think about the next in his hierarchy.

a) True
b) False

. . . .

Q13: Recognition is a true motivator.

a) True
b) False

. . . .

3.8 End of topic tests

End of topic 3 test

Q14: Match the type of training (1-3) with the appropriate definition (a-c).

Go online

1. Autocratic
2. Democratic
3. Laissez-faire

a) A leadership style where subordinates are given the freedom to make their own choices.
b) A leader who does not believe in giving responsibility to others.
c) A leader who believes in involving others in the decision making.

....

Q15: What is the most basic need according to Maslow?

a) Esteem
b) Safety
c) Physiological

....

Q16: What is the highest of Maslow's hierarchy of needs?

a) Esteem
b) Self-actualisation
c) Job enrichment

....

Q17: What was receiving a company car according to Herzberg?

a) Hygiene factor
b) Motivating factor

....

Q18: A democratic leader, who regularly delegates important decisions to staff, is more aligned with Theory Y.

a) True
b) False

....

Q19: McGregor believed managers either performed in the style of Theory X or Theory Y, but never both.

a) True
b) False

....

SQA style questions

Go online

Q20: Describe approaches used to motivate staff. (5 Marks)

....

Q21: Compare two theories of motivation. (2 Marks)

....

Topic 4

Employee relations

Contents

Learning objectives

After studying this topic, you should be able to:

- *describe the term 'employee relations';*

- *explain how policies (grievance, discipline) impact on employee relations;*

- *explain how contemporary working practices impact on employee relations;*

- *describe the positive impact of constructive employee relations;*

- *describe industrial action which can occur due to negative employee relations;*

- *describe the role of external institutions in the employee relations process;*

- *explain the impact of current employment legislation on employee relations.*

4.1   Employee relations

Employee relations are how employers deal with and interact with their employees as individuals or as a group.

Good employee relations will help ensure that the organisation meets its objectives.

Workers are:

- usually much happier;

- more motivated;

- committed to the goals of the business;

- more accepting of change;

- more flexible in their response to requests;

- more able to recognise the need for the organisation to achieve its objectives.

Poor employee relations will lead to:

- less cooperation of the workforce;

- more industrial action;

- a poor image for the organisation for its customers.

The HR department has responsibility for drawing up and implementing the organisations Employee Relations Policies. What they cover will vary with the organisation but should include:

- the terms and conditions of employment for staff;

- procedures for dealing with staff complaints (grievance);

- the procedures for disciplining of staff;

- redundancy - including any agreed payments;

- the involvement of staff in decision-making;

- trade Union recognition;

- collective bargaining - discussions with staff on pay and conditions or changes to working practices for all employees.

Identify which of the following statements are true and which are false.

Q1: Employee relations can affect the motivation of the workforce.

a) True
b) False

. . . .

Q2: Employee relations can affect the flexibility of the workforce.

a) True
b) False

. . . .

Q3: Poor employee relations will lead to less industrial action.

a) True
b) False

. . . .

Q4: Employee relations are about how managers interact with each other.

a) True
b) False

. . . .

Q5: Employee relations can affect the organisation's ability to achieve its objectives.

a) True
b) False

. . . .

Q6: Employee relations policy should not include a grievance procedure.

a) True
b) False

. . . .

Q7: Good employee relations policies will lead to greater staff turnover.

a) True
b) False

. . . .

Q8: Collective bargaining makes it more difficult for the organisation to come to an agreement with the employees.

a) True
b) False

. . . .

Q9: Employees relations policy should include and agreement about redundancy packages.

a) True
b) False

. . . .

Q10: Good employers don't recognise trade unions.

a) True
b) False

. . . .

4.2   Main institutions for employee relations

Because of the importance of achieving good employee relations a number of institutions have been created to help ensure that disputes between employers and employees are kept to a minimum.

ACAS - The Advisory, Conciliation and Arbitration Service.

They describe themselves as employee relations experts, helping people to work effectively together . The service offers advice setting up the right structures and systems for employee relations. It can also be involved in finding a way to settle disputes.

They spend most time advising on how to avoid disputes through good practice and dealing with individual cases.

There are four main ways that ACAS provides help.

1. Providing impartial information and help to anyone with a work problem.

2. Preventing and resolving problems between employers and their workforces, helping settle disputes.

3. Settling complaints about employees' rights.

4. Encouraging people to work together effectively by running workshops and seminars on basic employment issues and the latest developments in legislation.

Employer organisations

Businesses in one sector of industry often form an association to look after the interests of all businesses in that particular industry. They benefit from this association by having a single strong voice to lobby politicians, in their dealings with the engineering unions, and in dealing with the press and other media.

Market research can be gathered for the benefit of the members, many of whom may be small businesses, who would otherwise not be able to afford research.

Because of this training should be a continuous process for successful organisations.

1. **Confederation of British Industry - CBI**

   This body tries to represent the employers from all the UK's industries.

Employee organisations

1. **Trade Union Congress - TUC**

   The TUC represents all trade unions in much the same way as the CBI represents the employers. As with the CBI they provide information and advice to their members. Trade Union membership has seen a rise in membership in recent years after decades of decline. They are now more involved in research into employment and employment rights.

2. **Trade unions**

   They represent workers in their dealings with employers, and work to protect their rights and to improve their pay and conditions, and continue with their campaigns to introduce new laws that will protect and benefit working people.

   Individually workers have little power in their dealings with employers and government. However, by joining a trade union the worker has a much stronger voice and many more resources to make their point.

ACAS

Visit ACAS at http://www.acas.org.uk and find the 'ACAS model workplace'.

Write a short report of around 250 words explaining why ACAS believes that good employee relations are necessary for the success of the organisation.

Submit the finished report to your teacher.

4.3 Staff development and appraisal

Staff development is the process for helping employees to reach their full potential. It will include training, but to achieve full development some of the training will not be specific to the employee's existing job and will allow them to train in other areas and develop new skills.

Staff appraisal

The main method used for establishing an individual employee's training and development needs is through appraisal. Other uses for appraisals vary between organisations. They may, for example, be linked to pay.

They are meetings which take place on a one-to-one basis with the employee's line manager or a member of HR department. The purpose is to establish how the employee performed in their job, usually over the past year.

The process usually involves some preparation by both parties, and an end agreement on a set of goals for the employee. These goals will then form the basis of next year's appraisal, and so should be reviewed throughout the year to ensure they are being attained.

The main objectives for the organisation are:

- to identify future training needs;

- to consider development needs for the individual's career;

- to improve the performance of the employee;

- to provide positive feedback and constructive criticism for the employee about their performance;

- to identify individuals who have potential for future promotion within the organisation, or who have additional skills which could be useful now or in the future.

It is important that both sides take the appraisal process seriously by following proper processes. These include setting a date well in advance with an agenda and allowing good time for preparation of forms to be completed.

The employee should be encouraged to contribute effectively and so should not find the process threatening. The outcomes of the appraisal should be clear and any training needs identified with a course of action that includes appropriate training.

Q11: Staff appraisal should take place:

a)   at least once a week.
b)   at least once a month.
c)   at least once a year.
d)   when a new employee joins.

. . . .

Q12: The appraisal should be carried out by:

a)   the immediate subordinate.
b)   the line manager.
c)   a customer.
d)   the employee.

. . . .

Q13: The appraisal should identify:

a) training needs of the employee.
b) health needs of the employee.
c) child care needs of the employee.
d) income needs of the employee.

....

Q14: The appraisal should be used to:

a) discipline the employee.
b) demote the employee.
c) motivate the employee.
d) assess the performance of the employee.

....

Q15: Contributions to the appraisal should mostly be made by:

a) the employee alone.
b) the line manager alone.
c) both the employee and the line manager.
d) the employee's co-workers.

....

4.4   Employee relations processes

Types of employee relations processes

- **Negotiation**

  The purpose of negotiation is to come to an agreement. Here employers and employees will meet to discuss issues that affect both parties to agree, plan and implement some changes in the workplace.

- **Consultation**

  Consultation is enforced on employers under employment law for some changes within the organisation. No agreement is required and the employer is under no obligation to take account of the views of the employees.

- **Arbitration**

  Where no agreement can be reached between the employer and employees, and some form of industrial action is possible, an independent arbitrator such as ACAS may be called in to try to resolve the problem. The arbitrator is unbiased and neutral to the dispute and will listen to both sides and offer a solution.

- **Industrial tribunals**

  When all other avenues between employers and their employees have not settled a dispute, and for cases of unfair dismissal, the employee has the right to take their employer or former employer to an industrial tribunal. The tribunal is less formal than a court and aims to ensure that employers act legally in respect of the employment legislation.

Types of industrial action

- **Strikes**

  When the workers stop working. This stops production of goods and services meaning a loss of sales and customers.

- **Sit-in**

  Where workers occupy their workplace in an attempt to stop the employer closing the unit.

- **Work-to-rule**

  Where employees work strictly to their terms and conditions of employment.

- **Overtime ban**

  Where workers refuse to do overtime.

- **Boycotts**

  They can be used when employers introduce new machinery or duties that the employees disagree with. They simply refuse to carry out the new duties or use the new machines.

Costs of industrial action

For the Business

- Customers are unlikely to return if they are unable to purchase the product/speak to an employee to resolve an issue.
- Sales will be lost whilst work is stopped.
- Management is demotivated, which leads to further loss of activity.
- Relationships between employees and employers are damaged.

For the employee

- Employees are not paid for the time that they are on strike.
- Future orders may be affected, which could mean less hours/overtime available.
- Jobs could be lost if ling term damage is done to the business' reputation.

Employee relations

Q16: Complete the paragraph using following words.

Go online

| boycotts | arbitration | strikes | consult |
| negotiation | changes | agreement | unfairly |

The purpose of _____ is to come to an _____ between two or more parties. Employers are legally obliged to _____ their workers about some changes in the workplace. _____ is used when the parties cannot negotiate an agreement. Employment Tribunals are used by employees who have been allegedly _____ treated by their employer. _____ are where the employees stop working. _____ are used when the employees do not agree with _____ in the workplace.

. . . .

4.5 Management of employee relations

Businesses use a number of constructive policies and procedures to ensure employees receive a positive impact:

- **Counselling support**

  Businesses attempt to support staff by offering counselling services on a range of issues such as stress, health and careers. This might be undertaken by trained company staff; however, organisations are increasingly contracting external specialist counselling services who offer anonymous and confidential services, whilst ensuring the organisation is aware of the number of staff using the service in order to highlight stress levels.

- **Advice**

  Organisations will offer advice to employees on such matters as employment and health and safety legislation. Employees will have access to written company policies and procedures; however, it is also often necessary to provide explanation and advice on these areas. This can be done through Human Resources staff or trade union representatives. Examples of the types of advice most commonly offered are maternity and paternity rights, grievance and disciplinary procedures or rights to time off.

- **Grievance procedures**

  Organisations will normally have grievance and disciplinary procedures in place which aim to help resolve any difficulties between employer and employees within the workplace. Whilst disciplinary procedures deal with employee misconduct, grievance procedures provide a formal mechanism and support by which employees can take action if they feel they are being unfairly treated at work. This usually takes the form of a formal written document stating the different stages a grievance might go through, the personnel involved and the outcomes they can expect.

- **Return-to-work interviews**

  Most organisations will have policies on absence and illness and it is common for employees to receive advice and counselling upon returning to work after a prolonged absence. Many organisations operate a planned, gradual return to work for employees returning after extended absence and even use occupational health staff for support purposes.

- **Family-friendly policies**

  More and more organisations are realising the importance of flexibility in working practices. This includes supporting staff in balancing work and home responsibilities. Organisations have official policies and procedures in place for allowing such concessions as paid/unpaid paternity leave and time off for family events/issues. Some organisations even have what have become known as 'duvet-days' - these are days when staff may not be able to face the office for a number of reasons, but are not ill. Indeed, many organisations now operate flexi-time and hot-desking work practices where the emphasis isn't on 9 to 5 anymore, but on staff completing the required work.

- **Works council**

  This is a group of representatives from the workforce who have the legal right to access information from management and joint decision-making powers on most matters relating to employees.

- **Quality circles**

  These are groups of between 4-10 workers who work for the same supervisor. They meet regularly to identify, analyse, and attempt to solve work related problems. They increase the motivation of the workers by involving them in the decision-making around their own jobs, thus increasing efficiency and raising profitability.

- **Discipline procedures**

  Organisations should have written disciplinary procedures in place so that employees know what will happen if they break the organisational rules. These will state the process that will be followed when an employee has broken the rules. It will state the number of warnings that have to be given before dismissal is considered to be fair, and ensures that all employees are treated in the same way.

- **Redundancy**

  This is when the employer finds that they no longer require a number of their employees. Where this is the case the employer has to make redundancy payments to the employees and give them a certain amount of notice of the redundancy. The business cannot then employ other workers to do the job previously done by the workers made redundant as they would then have a claim for unfair dismissal.

- **Absenteeism**

  Employees who are absent without good reason, or where a pattern of absenteeism emerges, may have to attend absentee management meetings, where the business will work constructively with the employee to see if there is a reason for the continued absenteeism. The meetings should focus on the support available to the employee.

• **Downsizing and De-layering**

Downsizing is when a business chooses to reduce in size, perhaps to counter decreasing sales or an unsustainable branch or department. De-layering is when a business choses to reduce costs by removing a level of management. Any employee who finds themselves without a role as a result of downsizing or delayering will be offered an alternative role. Where this is not possible, redundancy may be offered. This is when an employee's contract is ended. The employee is usually remunerated (offered a sum of money) as part of the redundancy deal.

In addition, business may offer a number of 'extras' at work. These can include such benefits as corporate membership of health clubs, corporate cinema passes, 'employee of the month' rewards, or discounts at various outlets.

Radical solutions

Read the following article (http://www.bbc.co.uk/news/magazine-18826587) which examines eight possible solutions to the problem of childcare.

Choose the one method you think is best and write 100 words to justify your answer.

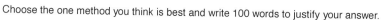

4.6 Dell

Dell

Dell is a US company that has grown rapidly since its formation 20 years ago and currently ranks number three on Fortune's Global Most Admired Companies list. It seeks to deliver value to customers through its direct business model, by focusing on the customer experience and taking out cost from the production process.

The company is data-driven. Managers report on the achievement of targets on a daily basis. Its employee relations climate is strongly influenced by its aspiration to be a 'great company and a great place to work' through the adoption of a 'winning culture'.

The focus is on the team and on individual contributions to the team. People/line managers are expected to interact with individuals, and their performance in this area is closely monitored. Both people managers and individual contributors are measured on the way in which they deal with people as well as on their technical proficiency. There's a consistent emphasis on how people do their job, not just what they do, including, for example, support for colleagues and behaving ethically.

The company makes a conscious effort to recruit people who will have a good 'fit' with its values - people who are open, direct and who focus on getting the job done rather than engaging in office politics. The company runs a leadership programme each year, which in 2013 focussed on personal development planning.

Employee engagement is driven by the relationship between individuals and their manager. The expectations of people managers are clearly defined:

- Set a performance plan
- Work in each team on individual development plans
- Undertake mid-year review
- Undertake end-year review
- Undertake monthly review with each individual
- Give feedback to improve performance

Dell measures people managers' compliance with their performance management targets, tracking what has been done at each stage. In addition, senior managers are expected to take regular opportunities to engage with more junior staff, for example, at 'brown bag' lunches with different groups, or while visiting operations in other countries, to help embed a common culture.

Q17: Dell describe themselves as a business that values employees.

a) True
b) False

....

Q18: Dell focussed on group management in 2013.

a) True
b) False

....

Q19: Dell are required by law to undertake monthly reviews with individual employees

a) True
b) False

....

Q20: Dell believe a positive corporate culture is important

a) True
b) False

....

Q21: Dell believe all countries should adopt the same corporate culture

a) True
b) False

....

4.7 Legislation

Employment law

> **Key point**
>
> The laws that an employer has to take account of are varied and complex. They are continually being updated. It is normally one of the main functions of the HR department to ensure that the organisation is fully aware of any legislation and to make sure it is implemented.
> There are two main areas:
>
> 1. Employment law
>
> 2. Health and safety at work

Employment law

Employment law exists to ensure employees are not discriminated against in any way. Examples of discrimination is usually in the form of age, gender, sexual orientation or religious beliefs. **The Equality Act 2010** exists to ensure no person is unfairly discriminated against. Prior to 2010, a large number of individual acts existed - primarily:

- the Equal Pay Act 1970;
- the Sex Discrimination Act 1975;
- the Race Relations Act 1976;
- the Disability Discrimination Act 1995.

The equality acts supersedes them all and requires equal treatment in access to employment in both public and private services, regardless of the protected characteristics of age, disability, gender, race, religion or belief, sex and sexual orientation. It brings all of these acts under the one piece of legislation.

Although the protected characteristics covered by discrimination legislation were not changed by the Act, there were significant changes to the law on disability discrimination. These are the result of shortfalls in protection highlighted by case law since the Disability Discrimination Act 1995 came into force.

The main changes were:

- Indirect discrimination applies to discrimination against disabled people.
- Associative discrimination applies to discrimination against disabled people.
- Perceptive discrimination applies to discrimination against disabled people.
- Discrimination arising from a disability is forbidden - this restores protection under the Discrimination Act 1995 which was lost as a result of case law.
- Pre-employment health questions are unlawful except for certain defined reasons.

Harassment is defined as: "unwanted conduct related to a relevant protected characteristic, which has the purpose or effect of violating an individual's dignity or creating an intimidating, hostile, degrading, humiliating or offensive environment for that individual".

Under the act employees can complain of harassment even if they don't possess the protected characteristic or the harassment is not directed at them.

Other employment law legislation are detailed below:

Employment Rights Act 1996	States the duties and rights of the employer and employee and includes the employees rights to maternity and paternity leave, termination of employment, the right to a written contract of employment within 60 days of starting work, Sunday working (England and Wales only), and the right to a written payslip.
Working Time Regulations Act 1998	Covers the maximum amount of time an employee can be expected to work; their entitlement to breaks and rest periods; the pattern of work; the length of time you can do night work; and their entitlement to leave.
Employment Act 2002	This act gives additional rights for things such as paternity leave, and an extension of some existing rights. Mothers and fathers of young children under six, or disabled children under 18, have a right to request a flexible working arrangement. It requires employers to have minimum internal disciplinary and grievance procedures to avoid the need for so many cases to go to industrial tribunals.
National Minimum Wage Act 1998	States the minimum wage that must be paid to employees. It is set on the recommendations of the Low Pay Commission, an expert panel made up of business figures, trade union leaders and academics.
Employment Relations Act 2004	This act deals mainly with employee relations and deals with the operation of the statutory recognition procedure for trade unions; the law on industrial action ballots and ballot notices; when arbitration should take place; unfair dismissal and grievance and disciplinary hearings.

Employment law

Categorise each sentence to the following acts.

Go online

- Employment Rights Act 1996

- Working Time Regulations Act 1998

- Employment Act 2002

- National Minimum Wage Act 1998

- Employment Relations Act 2004

- Equality Act 2010

Q22: This act ensures anyone over the age of 21 receives at least £6.31/hour.
....

Q23: Protected characteristics make sure nobody is discriminated against.
....

Q24: Maternity and paternity rights of mothers and fathers are detailed in this act.
....

Q25: You have rights if you decide to strike - this act makes sure.
....

Q26: You are entitled to a 15 minute break every 4 hours - this act says so!
....

Q27: Parents of disabled children where given more rights under this act.
....

4.8   Health and safety at work legislation

The main act here is the **Health and Safety at Work Act 1974** which includes the **Office, Shops and Railway Premises Act 1963**, although many of the other pieces of legislation affect health and safety in the workplace.

Employers duties:

- The employer must make sure that they take every reasonable step to ensure that all machinery is properly maintained.

- All hazardous substances are dealt with properly.

- All staff are trained and informed of potential dangers.

- The environment is safe and non-hazardous to the health of the employees.
- This will involve a 'Risk Assessment' of the building, operation of machinery, and of each task the employees are expected to carry out.
- They have to appoint safety officers and committees which will carry out regular inspections of the workplace and assess the dangers involved in each job.

Employees duties

- The employees are expected to behave in a reasonable manner at work and must take some responsibility for their own actions.
- They must cooperate with their employers in ensuring all health and safety requirements are met.
- They must follow all instructions and accept training were appropriate.

The act still includes many of the provisions of the earlier Office, Shops and Railway premises Act 1963 which covered minimum working temperatures, toilet facilities, first aid, physical space and levels of cleanliness.

The Office, Shops and Railway Premises Act covers things like working temperatures, toilet and washing facilities, space requirement for workers, cleanliness and first aid requirements.

Health and safety at work

Go online

Q28:

Complete the paragraph using following words.

reasonable	instructions	maintained	potential	inspection
trained	training	officers	actions	hazardous

All staff are _____ and informed of _____ dangers. Appoint safety _____ and committees which will carry out regular _____ of the workplace and assess the dangers involved in each job. The employer must make sure that they take every reasonable step to ensure that all machinery is properly _____ . All _____ substances are dealt with properly. The employees are expected to behave in a _____ manner at work and must take some responsibility for their own _____. Follow all _____ and accept _____ where appropriate.

. . . .

4.9 Summary questions

Summary questions

Q29: The purpose of employee relations is to deal with complaining workers.

Go online

a) True
b) False

....

Q30: Positive relations between employees and managers affects the amount of industrial action.

a) True
b) False

....

Q31: An employee must belong to a trade union before taking part in industrial action.

a) True
b) False

....

Q32: ACAS stands for Advice, Consideration and Arbitration Service.

a) True
b) False

....

Q33: Industrial tribunals independently review cases of unfair dismissal.

a) True
b) False

....

Q34: Overtime ban is when employees only work their contracted hours.

a) True
b) False

....

Q35: Strikes increase productivity.

a) True
b) False

....

Q36: Quality circles involve workers sitting in a circle and discussing managers.

a) True
b) False

. . . .

Q37: A grievance is a complaint by an employee against a manager.

a) True
b) False

. . . .

Q38: Organisations must have a written disciplinary procedure.

a) True
b) False

. . . .

Q39: Indirect discrimination is illegal under the Equality Act 2012.

a) True
b) False

. . . .

Q40: The Equality Act 2010 supersedes other discrimination acts.

a) True
b) False

. . . .

Q41: A person's nationality is a protected characteristic.

a) True
b) False

. . . .

Q42: Harassment is defined as: "Unwanted conduct related to a relevant protected characteristic".

a) True
b) False

. . . .

Q43: The business is solely responsible for an employee's health and safety.

a) True
b) False

. . . .

4.10 End of topic tests

End of topic 4 test

For each definition select an appropriate service.

Go online

- Advisory

- Conciliation

- Arbitration

Q44: A final decision on a course of action when all other attempts to reconcile have failed.

. . . .

Q45: To give impartial advice on a number of matters.

. . . .

Q46: To reconcile two parties who are at odds with the aim of bringing agreement.

. . . .

Q47: Match the Trade Union with the industry it represents.

1. EIS	a) Journalists
2. FBU	b) Teachers
3. NUJ	c) Flight attendants
4. PFA	d) Footballers
5. AFA	e) Public sector workers
6. Unisor	f) Fire fighters

. . . .

Q48: From the following list correctly identify the 9 protected characteristics from the **Equality Act 2010**.

- Height
- Weight
- Disability
- Pregnancy and maternity
- Age
- Religion or belief
- Nationality
- Sex
- Sexual orientation
- Race
- Marriage and civil partnership
- Gender reassignment
- Political preference
- Food preferences

. . . .

Go online

SQA style questions

Q49: Explain the importance of employee relations policy to an organisation. (4 Marks)

. . . .

Q50: Describe what should be contained in the organisation's employee relations policy. (4 Marks)

. . . .

Q51: Describe ways an organisation could encourage positive employee relations. (4 Marks)

. . . .

Q52: Describe the impact of the Equality Act 2010 on organisations and employees. (4 Marks)

. . . .

Topic 5

Sources of finance

Contents

Learning objectives

After studying this topic, you should be able to:

- *justify the suitability of different sources of finance for large organisations;*

- *describe internal and external sources;*

- *compare external long-term and external short-term sources;*

- *explain factors for selecting sources of finance.*

5.1 Sources of finance

> **Key point**
>
> Organisations require finance to survive and to expand. This finance can be short-term, to pay a wages shortfall or cover the cost of purchasing raw materials whilst waiting on a **debtor** to repay a loan, or long-term, to fund an expansion strategy or to purchase an large piece of machinery or warehouse. Successful businesses use profit made to finance their business. All businesses may require additional finances to stay afloat or grow.

Banks

Banks (high street and commercial, broadly dealing with the general public and large companies respectively) are a **useful** source of information and finance to businesses.

They are able to provide services such as:

- Financial advice
- Business planning
- Legal assistance
- Other general business and financial services

Banks are able to provide both short and long-term sources of finance. For example, an overdraft facility may be required to overcome a short-term cash flow crisis (for example, whilst waiting for customers to pay a supplier) or a long-term loan may be required to finance the purchase of new assets for the business. Most bank loans are considered to be medium-term sources of finance.

Venture Capitalist

This is an individual or business that agrees to loan an amount of money to another business (similar to a bank). Venture capitalists tend to loan to businesses that banks deem to be too risky. For that reason they charge higher rates of interests and are usually only interested in large loans. They are a long-term source of finance.

Mortgages

Mortgages are long-term sources of finance provided by banks, building societies and other lenders. They are used to purchase buildings. The rate of interest is linked to the Bank of England base rate, meaning that it can increase or decrease over the period of the loan. The loan is normally paid back over 15 - 30 years. The property belongs to the lender until the full loan and interest is repaid. They are long-term sources of finance.

Overdraft

An overdraft is a short-term source of finance. It is used when a business identifies a shortfall in cash (for example, a bill is due and the business has insufficient funds to pay the bill). It is simple to arrange and cheap and the amount borrowed can vary up to the maximum agreed. Interest will only be charged on the amount of the overdraft that is used. It can, however, be expensive if used for a long period of time and it can be recalled (i.e. you can be asked to pay it back) with little notice.

Retained profits

Some businesses may opt to use profits from previous years to self-finance their business. The benefit of this method of finance is that there is no associated cost. However, organisations that use retained profits often do not have sufficient levels of finance in order to grow quickly.

Leasing

This method of finance is often used to finance fixed assets. The assets are rented for a fixed period of time e.g. office equipment or cars. At the end of the lease the assets are returned. Disadvantages are that the assets are never owned and the rental charges may be high.

Debentures

These are used as a source of long-term finance by public limited companies. A debenture is a loan or group of loans usually secured on the assets of the company. Interest is charged over the period of the loan and the initial sum borrowed is paid back at the end. The debenture interest must be paid even when the company makes a loss and if the business fails, the debenture holder will have the right to take the company's assets.

Sale of assets

Businesses requiring additional capital may need to sell unnecessary assets. This is a short-term source of finance as an asset can only be sold once. A business must be sure that it no longer needs the asset, as production and therefore profits may suffer in the future if the asset is crucial to the operation of the business.

Share issue

This source of finance is available to private and public limited companies. When a business makes the decision to issue shares for sale they reduce the importance of existing shares. They must have the agreement of existing shareholders before further shares can be issued. If this agreement is granted, shares are offered to individuals (in the case of Private Limited Companies) or made publicly available on the stock market (in the case of Public Limited Companies). In return for their investment, shareholders receive an annual payment (known as a dividend and similar to a bank paying out interest). Businesses only receive finance once - when the shares are first purchased. If shares are later resold it is the owning shareholder who benefits.

Debt factoring

A debt factor is a business that buys the debt off of another business for less than the value of the debt. It then attempts to recover the full debt from the debtor. This means that the business selling the debt receives most of the cash they need more quickly, and the business buying the debt make a profit when they recover the full amount.

5.2   Factors for selecting sources of finance

Businesses require finance at different times and for many different reasons. The most important factor is deciding why the finance is required in the first place. If a small amount of money is required, or for a short period of time, then a business may request a bank overdraft to cover the shortfall. Trade credit (where a business purchases stock and pays later) is another useful **short term** source of finance. Factoring and retained profits are considered short-term as the method can only be used once. Once the money, or debt, has been used, or repaid, it is gone.

Bank loans, leasing and hire purchase (where a deposit is paid on the purchase 'of an asset with the remaining balance being paid off over time) are **medium-term** sources of finance. When using one these sources a business must consider the interest being charged and the length of time the agreement is in place for.

Long-term sources of finance include share issue, debentures and venture capitalists. Again, businesses must consider the interest being charged and the length of time the agreement is in place for. A longer term means less monthly repayments but a bigger amount of interest overall. Businesses must also realise that when they issue shares or use venture capitalists they have to be prepared to give up part ownership of their business in return for the investment.

Go online

Sources of finance

Q1: For each finance source given, decide if it is:

- long-term
- medium-term
- short-term.

1. Hire purchase
2. Trade credit
3. Debentures
4. Grant
5. Retained profits
6. Leasing
7. Venture capital
8. Owner's savings (new capital)
9. Debt factoring
10. Bank loan
11. Overdraft
12. New issue of shares

. . . .

5.3   Summary questions

Q2: An overdraft is more appropriate than a bank loan as a long-term source of finance.

a) True

b) False

. . . .

Q3: During a recession a firm that has many shareholders and no bank loans is likely to be in a better financial position than one which has a few shareholders and high bank loans.

a) True
b) False

. . . .

Q4: An advantage of selling shares is that the original owners retain full control.

a) True
b) False

. . . .

Q5: A mortgage is a suitable long-term source of finance for acquiring new premises.

a) True
b) False

. . . .

Q6: Sole traders often finance capital expenditure by borrowing from family members.

a) True
b) False

. . . .

Q7: Venture capitalists sometimes provide finance for risky ventures that they believe in in return for a stake in the business concerned.

a) True
b) False

. . . .

Q8: Sale and leaseback agreements do nothing to improve a firm's cash flow in the short run.

a) True
b) False

. . . .

Q9: Debentures are loans repaid to other companies.

a) True
b) False

. . . .

5.4   End of topic tests

End of topic 5 test

Go online

Q10: Match the sources of finance (1-8) with the definitions (a-h).

1. Source
2. Overdraft
3. Trade credit
4. Debt factor
5. Retained profit
6. Share issue
7. Debentures
8. Venture capitalist

a) Selling your debt to another business.
b) Limited companies sell a percentage of their business in return for an investment.
c) A group of loans that pays monthly interest and the full loan at the end of the term.
d) Definition.
e) Money that a business makes and keeps for use in the future.
f) An individual or business that invests in a riskier business for a higher return on their investment.
g) Bank allows you to withdraw more money than you have in your account.
h) Buying purchases and paying later.

. . . .

Categorise the following sources of finance as **external** or **internal**.

Q11:

- Venture capital
- Hire purchase
- Retained profit
- Debentures
- Bank loan
- Bank overdraft
- Leasing
- Share issue
- Owner's savings
- Debt factoring

Internal	External

....

For each problem, identify an appropriate source of finance.

Q12: The banking group TSB is looking for members of the public to invest in them in return for an annual divided.

a) Overdraft
b) Share issue
c) Venture capital

....

Q13: A business is looking to purchase a fleet of vans but does not have the upfront capital required.

a) Retained profits
b) Overdraft
c) Leasing

....

Q14: "We've a large cheque coming in three days, but we need to pay our staff tomorrow."

a) Debentures
b) Leasing
c) Overdraft

. . . .

Q15: "We saved for a rainy day!"

a) Bank loan
b) Retained profit
c) Venture capital

. . . .

Q16: "We've made a loss, but we still need to pay this back."

a) Debentures
b) Share issue
c) Grant

. . . .

Go online

SQA style questions

Q17: Describe possible sources of finance for a private limited company looking to expand its activities. (5 Marks)

. . . .

Topic 6

Cash budgeting

Contents

Learning objectives

After studying this topic, you should be able to:

- *describe the purpose of budgeting as an aid to decision making;*

- *interpret cash budgets as a means of solving cash flow issues.*

6.1 Budgets

> **Key point**
>
> A budget is simply a statement of anticipated future expenditure. It will usually cover a specific time period e.g. a month or a year. Budgets are usually financial in nature although they can be expressed in other ways.

A simple cash budget for a small business is shown below.

Cash budget for Hislop Computer Services

	January	February	March
	£	£	£
Opening balance	3700	6140	5975
Cash in			
Product sales - cash	800	300	350
Repair sales - cash	1300	1100	600
Product sales - credit	2800	1200	800
Total cash in	4900	2600	1750
Cash out			
Cash purchases	1200	1500	2400
Wages	650	650	650
Insurance	200	200	200
Rent	350	350	350
Telephone	60	65	43
Total cash out	2460	2765	3643
Closing balance	6140	5975	4082

What can we tell from this budget?

- We can see that the closing balance is falling each month. If this continues then the business could end up with no cash to pay its bills.

- The sales are falling each month - this could be due to competition, or because February and March are times of year when sales are slow.

- The payment for purchases are increasing each month - this may be because of credit sales for which the money will be paid later in the year, or because of rising prices from suppliers.

- Wages, rent, and insurance remain constant each month.

Because management have drawn up the budget in advance, they can do something to overcome any problems.

They could:

- spend money on advertising to try and increase sales;
- try to find new suppliers who will offer lower prices;
- try to buy the supplies on credit;
- buy fewer supplies;
- use fewer staff during quiet periods.

Cash budget: Hislop Computers

Write a report on the effect that the following changes would make on the cash budget for Hislop Computer Services.

Go online

Hislop Cash Budget

	January	February	March
	£	£	£
Opening balance	3700	6140	5975
Cash in			
Product sales - cash	800	300	350
Repair sales - cash	1300	1100	600
Product sales - credit	2800	1200	800
Total cash in	4900	2600	1750
Cash out			
Cash purchases	1200	1500	2400
Wages	650	650	650
Insurance	200	200	200
Rent	350	350	350
Telephone	60	65	43
Advertising	0	0	0
Total cash out	2460	2765	3643
Closing balance	6140	5975	4082

Base your report on the following changes:

- Spending money on advertising.
- Changing a supplier to one who charges 10% less.
- Taking up the option of taking 1 month's credit from the existing supplier who would then add a delivery charge of 5% .
- Reducing staff costs by £150 per month by closing at lunch time.

Conclude your report with the decisions you would take.

When you are finished show your work to your teacher for feedback.

. . . .

6.2   Budgets and management

Budgets are an essential management tool to:

- **Monitor and control:** Setting a budget and then comparing it to actual performance means that comparisons can be made on a regular basis and changes adopted quickly to remedy problems.

- **Gain information:** Budgets allow managers to see how well the business is performing.

- **Set targets:** This gives managers and employees limits to reach.

- **Delegate authority:** The use of budgets means that managers can give responsibility to employees.

Cash budgets are a common type of budget that are used by most businesses to monitor, control, obtain and present information. They can be used to monitor the cash position of a particular department, section or project or the business as a whole. They can also be used as a management decision making tool to assess the validity of a particular project or scenario. A cash projection may be used as part of a submission to a lender to secure finance.

The main benefits to management of using cash budgets can be summarised as:

- **Planning:** Look ahead to set aims and strategies. This allows problems solving to be planned rather than having to react to situations as they happen.

- **Organisation:** Allows the right resources to be in the right place at the right time.

- **Command:** When management are able to make informed decisions, this enables them to instruct their subordinates. The management will have access to all the budgets for each department which will be fed into the master budget e.g. the cash budget.

- **Co-ordinate:** Management can give instructions to those in charge of departmental budgets and keep a clear overview of the business as a whole.

- **Control:** Evaluation and review of budgets allows management to exert control over the organisation as a whole.

- **Delegation:** Management should make subordinates responsible for a suitable range of and give them the authority to carry them out.

- **Motivation:** Management have a responsibility to motivate their staff. This can be done through setting realistic targets in the budgets and introducing concepts and practices such as team work, empowerment and incentives for meeting targets or operating within budget.

Cash budget: Winmill Confectionery

Q1: Study the cash budget showing the first 6 months of the year for Winmill Confectionery.

Go online

Cash budget for Winmill Confectionery

	Jan	Feb	Mar	Apr	May	Jun
	£	£	£	£	£	£
Opening balance	15400	13100	11400	11300	-8200	-9500
Cash in						
Shop sales	8500	9100	6700	12000	13000	17500
Wholesale	16000	16000	20000	20000	20000	28000
Contract sales	13500	13500	13500	800	14500	14500
Total cash in	38000	38600	40200	32800	47500	60000
Cash out						
Materials	12000	12000	12000	24000	20000	20000
Wages	17500	17500	17500	17500	17500	17500
Rent	1000	1000	1000	1000	1500	1500
Insurance	1200	1200	1200	1200	1200	1200
Telephone	130	130	130	130	130	130
Administration expenses	2300	2300	2300	2300	2300	2300
Distribution expenses	6000	6000	6000	6000	6000	6000
Power	170	170	170	170	170	170
Total cash out	40300	40300	40300	52300	48800	48800
Closing balance	13100	11400	11300	-8200	-9500	1700

In April and May the closing cash balance is negative. Write a paragraph to describe what actions the management of Winmill could take to avoid problems in these months.

In addition, consider the effect that one of the following changes would make to the cash budget:

1. A new supplier has been found who can offer materials at a reduction of 10% of existing costs. The new supplier will be used from January onwards.
2. The shop landlord has informed Winmill that rent will increase by 50% from February.
3. A new restaurant opening in February have signed a contract worth £800 per month.
4. The management have agreed a pay rise for employees of 10% to take effect in March.

When you are finished show your work to your teacher or tutor for feedback.

Note: In reality a combination of changes may be made and the order of implementation of such changes will affect the overall cash budget.

If you have time you can experiment with making combinations of these changes.

....

6.3   Cash flow management

Cash and cash management are the most important aspects of business.

Without cash, the business will fail.

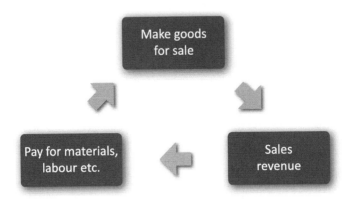

The business needs cash to pay for the following:

- Suppliers
- Wages and salaries
- Telephone
- Electricity

If they cannot pay these suppliers will stop supplying, workers will stop working, the telephone will be cut off, there will be no power - in other words the business will not be able to operate and will therefore fail.

Q2:   Apart from those above, identify five other regular payments that a taxi firm would have to make.

. . . .

The concept of cash flow is about liquidity - the ability to meet the everyday bills of the business.

Cash flow management is about the movement of money in and out of the business. The following terms are used:

- **Cash inflow** - a movement of cash into the business - money in.
- **Cash outflow** - a movement of cash out of the business - money out.

Consider a business manufacturing paints:

Q3:   Which of the following will be a cash inflow for the company?

a) Purchase of tins for the paint.
b) Sale of a small warehouse.
c) Buying raw materials.
d) Servicing a loan.

. . . .

Q4:   Which will be a cash outflow?

a) Building a factory extension.
b) Receipts from sales.
c) New capital investment.
d) Company profits.

. . . .

6.4   Cash flow problems

There are several reasons why a successful business might encounter cash flow problems:

- Buying fixed assets which are not needed.

- Buying too much stock which then takes time to sell.

- Allowing customers too long to pay/debtor collection period is too long.

- Slow-paying customers.

- Debtors who fail to pay at all - bad debts.

- Lack of forward planning.

- High level of drawings by the owners/dividends too high.

- High interest rates on loans.

- Lower than expected sales due to external factors.

Solving cash flow problems

Some problems are within the organisation's control. If it plans properly and takes account of possible problems in the future, these can be avoided.

So, good cash flow management policies can be adopted to avoid problems which can force the business to fail.

Some of the problems are outwith the control of the business, however, there is a number of actions that can be taken to overcome short-term cash flow problems:

- They could sell assets that are no longer needed, or sell their assets to a finance company and lease them back.

- They could offer discounts to encourage cash sales and offer promotions to reduce the levels of stock if they are too high.

- They could take actions to encourage or force slow paying customers to pay up, or sell their debts to a debt factor (banks offer this service), who will give them a percentage of the value of the invoices.

- The owners could increase the amount of capital in the business, and withdraw less cash from the business.

- They could adopt cost saving measures, even making some staff redundant.

- They could arrange cheaper finance with lenders or better credit terms with their suppliers.

Whichever actions they decide to use, they must be effective in improving the liquidity of the business or the business will fail.

6.5   Summary question

Go online

Summary question

Q5: A decrease in creditors will improve cashflow.

a) True
b) False

....

Q6: Sale of stock will improve cashflow.

a) True
b) False

....

Q7: Lack of forward planning causes cashflow issues.

a) True
b) False

....

Q8: Cash flow deals with a business's liquidity.

a) True
b) False

....

Q9: Business budgets only deal with cash.

a) True
b) False

....

6.6 End of topic tests

End of topic 6 test

Complete the paragraph using following words.

Go online

| managers | budget | sales | outflows |
| an overdraft | profit | debtors | expenses |

Q10: Companies need to _____ and be aware of cash flow in order to stay solvent. Cash flow is the movement of money in and out of the business. Cash flows out when _____ are paid and cash flows into the business when _____ are made. _____ and cash flow are two very different things. Cash flow is simply about money coming and going from the business. The challenge for _____ is to make sure there is always enough cash to pay expenses when they are due, as running out of cash threatens the survival of the business. A business can improve its cash flow by reducing cash _____ , e.g. by delaying the payment of bills, securing better trade credit terms or factoring. Increasing cash inflows can happen by chasing _____ , selling assets or securing _____ .

....

SQA style questions

Q11: Describe reasons for cash flow problems that can affect an organisation. (4 Marks)

Go online

....

Q12: Describe the advantages/disadvantages of budgets as a planning tool. (9 Marks)

....

Topic 7

Financial statements

Contents

Learning objectives

After studying this topic, you should be able to:

- *describe the purpose, main elements and interpretation of an income statement (trading and profit and loss account);*

- *describe the purpose, main elements and interpretation of the statement of financial position (balance sheet);*

- *identify users of financial information and justify what they use it for.*

Due to changes to UK Financial Reporting language, some financial terms are changing. For sessions 2014/15 and 2015/16 both the old and new terms are acceptable. Scholar notes will use the new terminology (with the current terminology in brackets).

7.1   Maintenance of financial records

All companies are required to maintain financial records. They are an essential part of the business as they show the history of all the business's activities and provide the basis for internal control, internal reporting, and external reporting to agencies such as the HM revenue and customs.

The HM Revenue and Customs requires that businesses retain financial records and related documents for a period of 6 years for the purpose of possible investigation. It is an offence not to do this.

Limited companies are required to keep records under the Companies Act of 2006 where it states that it is an offence not to maintain proper financial records. The Act also states that Public Limited Companies must publish these accounts on their website. Private Limited Companies do not.

These records form the basis of many business decisions and without proper financial records, managers would not make correct decisions and the business would not be able to operate effectively or efficiently.

Financial information

Financial information may be presented by a business in different formats. For example, the business will have different formats for information that is used internally and information that is presented externally.

There are two main financial statements that all businesses use:

1. **Income statement (Trading, Profit and Loss Account)**

2. **Statement of financial position (Balance Sheet)**

7.2   The income statement (Trading, profit and loss account)

The trading section of the income statement shows the gross profit of the business. The gross profit is the profit before any of the business's expenses are taken into account and it gives an indication of the business's trading performance.

It shows the difference between how much money the business generates from selling (sales) and how much the goods it is selling actually cost i.e. cost of sales.

An example of a simple income statement would look like this:

Ellis & Ross Income Statement for year ending 31 December 20xx

	£	£
Turnover/net sales		230000
Cost of sales		
Opening stock of goods	40000	
Purchases	90000	
	130000	
Less closing stock of goods	(50000)	80000
Gross profit		**150000**

A simple income statement

You can see that this account details the contribution of turnover/net sales, opening stock of goods, purchases and closing stock to the gross profit.

The income statement is used by businesses as both a statement for internal and external reporting. The profit and loss account used for internal reporting may be produced on a monthly basis and go into great detail, whereas the profit and loss account that is produced as a statutory requirement at the end of the financial year will contain much less detail in the information as they will want to keep details away from competitors.

The profit and loss account shows the business income and expenses over the course of the financial year. The money spent by the business is compared to the money earned, and where the business income is greater than the expenditure, a net profit is recorded. On the other hand, where the business expenditure is greater than the income, a loss is recorded.

It is important that the business properly matches its income and expenditure for the period for which the income statement is drawn up, and this is a requirement of accounting conventions. This ensures that the profit (or loss) calculated is accurate and is a true reflection of the business's trading activities.

Ellis & Ross income statement for the year ending 31 December 20xx

	£	£
Gross profit		150000
Other operating income		
Loan interest received	2000	2000
		152000
Expenses		
Wages	50000	
Advertising	5000	
Administration expenses	12000	
Logistics	15000	
Insurance	3000	
Electricity	6000	
Telephone	1000	92000
Net profit		**60000**

Income statement

A more complicated format of the income statement is used for limited companies. Limited companies must comply with the requirements of the Companies Act 2006 and so their year end accounts must be prepared in accordance with the formats prescribed by the law.

All other types of business will produce a similar type of income statement but it will usually be less detailed than that required by the limited company.

Here is an example of an income statement for a limited company.

Hill and Oakes Ltd
Income statement for the year ending 31 December 20xx

	£	£
Turnover		6900000
Cost of goods sold		2000000
Gross profit		4900000
Operating expenses	250000	
Other operating Income	160000	
Net operating expenses		900000
Operating profit		4,000000
Investment income		200000
Net profit before interest payable		4,200000
Interest payable		150000
Profit on ordinary activities before tax		4050000
Corporation tax		750000
Profit on ordinary activities after tax		3300000
Preference dividend		300000
Profit attributable to ordinary shareholders		3000000
Ordinary dividend	500000	
Transfer to reserves	1500000	2000000
Unappropriated profit for this year		1000000
Balance brought forward		1500000
Balance carried forward		**2500000**

Income statement for a limited company

The type of income statement that is produced will depend on the type of business e.g. sole trader, partnership, private limited company or public limited company. This type of account contains values for corporation tax, dividend and unappropriated profit.

Profits may be distributed in a number of different ways:

- Payment of corporation tax

- Payment of a dividend to shareholders

- Appropriated amongst the business partners

- Retained in the business

Coulter: Income statement

Go online

Q1: Complete the income statement for Coulter for the year ending 31 March using the information given.

	£
bank interest	2000
office expenses	12000
closing stock of goods	(60000)
wages	35000
purchases	85000
telephone	5000
opening stock of goods	70000
advertising	4000
heat and light	9000
carriage out	3000
rent received	4000

	£	£
turnover		220000
cost of sales		
opening stock of goods		
purchases		
less closing stock of goods		
gross profit		125000
other operating profit		
rent received		
expenses		
wages		
carriage out		
office expenses		
advertising		
telephone		
heat and light		
bank interest		
Net profit		

. . . .

7.3   Statement of financial position (Balance sheet)

The income statement records a history of the business activity throughout the financial year but the statement of financial position is a picture of the business at a point in time - normally at the end of the financial year.

It shows the financial worth and the financial position of the business at a particular point in time.

For this reason, the statement of financial position of any company is out of date by the time it is published. It forms part of the historic accounting records of the business.

The statement of financial position details three different pieces of information about the business:

- Assets

- Liabilities

- Capital

The statement of financial position has two parts. The first part of the statement of financial position shows the assets and liabilities of the business. Assets are things that the business owns either for the long term (fixed assets) or for the short term (current assets). Liabilities are the things that the business owes money for. They can be either current liabilities or long-term liabilities.

Fixed assets are needed within the business. Without these assets, the business would not be able to function on a day-to-day basis. These are things like buildings, machinery and other equipment.

Current assets are assets that change on a daily basis and can be turned easily into cash. Examples of current assets are money in the bank, stocks of goods and debtors.

Current liabilities (creditors falling due within one year) are also listed on the top half of the statement of financial position and are shown as a deduction from current assets. This is because the business will (eventually) turn all of its current assets into cash and subsequently use this cash to pay its current liabilities.

These liabilities are known as current because they will normally have to be repaid within a period of 12 months. The most common example of a current liability is creditors i.e. people or other businesses to whom the business owes money for goods or services supplied on credit.

The difference between the total current assets and the total current liabilities is highlighted on the statement of financial position. This is known as Working capital or Net current assets. This figure is extremely important because it highlights the business's ability to meet its short-term debts. This figure should normally always be positive.

Where the Net Current Assets figure is negative the company is in potential financial difficulty as it may not be able to pay its debts. This does not mean that the business is not profitable, however it does mean that it has liquidity problems.

Most businesses fail due to liquidity problems and it is one of the main functions of the finance department to make sure that there is always sufficient cash to pay it short-term debts.

Long-term liabilities (sometimes called creditors falling due after more than one year) are listed in the first part of the statement of financial position after net current assets. These are liabilities that the business must repay after more than one year. Examples include debentures and other longer-term loans.

The total of fixed assets plus the net current assets minus long-term liabilities is known as the business's net worth. This means the *value* of the business in monetary terms on the particular date specified on the statement of financial position.

The Net Worth of the statement of financial position is also expressed by calculating the opening capital invested by the owner and adding any profit accrued in the last year. Once long term liabilities, such as loans and mortgages, are deducted the Net Worth is calculated. This should equate to the working capital figure. In other words, the statement of financial position should 'balance'.

Q2:   Which of the following would be a fixed asset for Scotsman Newspapers Ltd?

a) Loans on their premises
b) Payments for Printing Inks
c) Printing Presses
d) Stocks of Paper

. . . .

Q3:   Which would be current assets?

a) Loans on their premises
b) Payments for Printing Inks
c) Printing Presses
d) Stocks of Paper

. . . .

Q4:   Which would be current liabilities?

a) Loans on their premises
b) Payments for Printing Inks
c) Printing Presses
d) Stocks of Paper

. . . .

Q5: Which would be long-term liabilities?

a) Loans on their premises
b) Payments for Printing Inks
c) Printing Presses
d) Stocks of Paper

. . . .

Q6: In the equation:
Total fixed assets + Net current assets - Long-term liabilities = X
what does X represent?

. . . .

The second part of the statement of financial position represents the capital side of the accounting equation. This is the amount of money invested by the owner(s)/shareholders. It also contains the reserves, which are money and profits retained in the business and not paid out to the owners.

The two parts of the statement of financial position must balance - i.e. the totals at the bottom of each must be equal.

An example of a statement of financial position follows:

Smith and Ross Ltd.
Statement of financial position as at 31 December 2014

	£000	£000	£000
Fixed assets			
Premises		2300	
Machinery		600	
Delivery vehicles		250	
			3150
Current assets			
Stocks	500		
Debtors	700		
Cash at bank	250	1450	
Creditors liabilities			
Creditors	400		
Tax	100		
Ordinary dividends	200	700	
Net current assets			750
Total assets less current liabilities			2400
Long-term liabilities			
Creditors due in > one year			
Mortgage		100	
Debentures (5%)		1200	1,300
Net assets			1100
	£000	£000	£000
Capital and reserves			
Ordinary share capital		900	
Retained profits		400	
Net worth			**1100**

Lawrenson: Statement of financial position

Q7: Complete the statement of financial position for Lawrenson Ltd.

Go online

	£
creditors	700
delivery vehicles	200
tax	100
machinery	500
ordinary share capital	3000
debentures (5%)	400
ordinary dividends	300
cash at bank	200
fixtures and fittings	300
retained profits	500
stocks	400
bank loan	500

Statement of financial position

	£000	£000	£000
Fixed assets		3300	
premises			
machinery			
delivery vehicles			
Current assets			
Debtors	600		
Stocks			
Cash at bank			
Current liabilities			
Creditors			
Ordinary dividends			
Tax			
Net current assets			
Total assets less current liabilities			
Long-term liabilities			
Bank loan			
Debentures (5%)			
Net assets			
Capital and reserves			
Ordinary share capital			
Retained profits			
Net assets			

. . . .

7.4   Users of financial information

Different people will use financial information for different reasons. Internal users, such as owners and managers will want to know that there is sufficient cash flow to pay suppliers; employees will want to know that there wages will be paid on time and shareholders will look to see the return they expect to see on their investment. External users, such as banks, will want to know that any loan can be repaid; the HM revenue and customs may examine financial records to ensure the correct level of taxation is being paid and Suppliers will want to know that they will be paid on time.

Users of financial information

Q8:

Go online

Match the user of financial information (1-6) with the use (a-f).

1. Bank
2. Shareholders
3. HM revenue and customs
4. Local community
5. Managers
6. Suppliers

a) Need to make sure that payments for goods purchased will be met.
b) Interested in making sure the business is paying the correct amount of taxation.
c) Interested in the profitability to ensure the business provides employment in the future.
d) Looks at projected cash flow to ensure loan repayments are met.
e) Looks at projected profit to see if dividends will be paid.
f) Looks at projected profit to see if bonuses will be paid.

. . . .

7.5 Summary questions

Summary questions

Q9: Which assets does the business need to continue to run?

a) Net assets
b) Net current assets
c) Fixed assets
d) Current assets

Go online

....

Q10: What shows the business performance in buying and selling goods?

a) Statement of financial position
b) Trading account
c) Income statement
d) Cost of sales

....

Q11: What shows the difference between Gross profit and Net profit?

a) Investment income
b) Unappropriated profit
c) Expenses
d) Dividends

....

Q12: Which of these are long-term liabilities for the business?

a) Mortgage
b) Debtors
c) Reserves
d) Bank loan

a) a
b) a; c
c) a; d
d) b; c; d

....

Q13: Name the revenue the business receives from trading.

a) Purchases
b) Turnover
c) Stock
d) Taxation

....

Q14: What shows the ability of the business to pay its short-term debts?

a) Cash
b) Sales
c) Dividends
d) Working capital

. . . .

Q15: Which of the following are the responsibility of the finance function?

a) Payment of wages
b) Increasing sales
c) Monitoring of funds
d) Arranging carriage on sales

a) a; c
b) a; d
c) b; c
d) All of them

. . . .

Q16: Which of the following are internal users of financial information?

a) Banks
b) Shareholders
c) Trade unions
d) Managers

a) b
b) a; b; d
c) b; c; d
d) b; d

. . . .

Q17: Which two figures need to be equal in the statement of financial position?

a) Net Profit and Net Assets
b) Net Assets and Net Worth
c) Net Worth and Net Profit
d) Gross Profit and Net Profit

. . . .

Q18: Name the owner(s) investment in the business.

a) Working Capital
b) Retained Profit
c) Capital
d) Debentures

. . . .

7.6   End of topic tests

End of topic 7 test

Q19: Complete the table using the following terms.

Go online

Retained profit	Sales revenue	Current liabilities	Creditors
Electricity	Fixed assets	Gross profit	Cost of sales
Net worth	Net sales	Bank	Rent

Income statement	Statement of financial position

....

Q20: Complete the paragraph using following words.

| profit | bonuses | overdrafts | revenue | suppliers |
| shareholders | wages | flow | private | creditors |

Potential _____ are interested in a public limited companies financial accounts to see if the return on investment will be high enough. They can find this information on the Internet. There are other external users, such as _____ , who will be interested to make sure their goods are paid for on time. Banks will want to make sure that cash _____ will be sufficient enough to see _____ being repaid and _____ will want to make sure that they are paid promptly for the money they are owed. Only internal users have access to accounts in a _____ limited company. Owners will try and make predications based on past performance. They will look at previous sales _____ , gross and net _____ and expenses. Employees will want to see that their _____ will be paid, whilst managers will be interested in performance related _____ .

....

SQA style questions

Q21: Describe financial statements that potential shareholders could use to decide whether or not to invest in a company. (5 Marks)

Go online

....

Q22: Describe the role of the finance department in meeting the expectations of HMRC (Inland Revenue). (2 Marks)

....

Topic 8

Ratio analysis

Contents

Learning objectives

After studying this topic, you should be able to:

- *explain the purpose of ratio analysis;*

- *describe the limitations of ratio analysis;*

- *justify the use of profitability, liquidity and efficiency ratios to make evaluative comments on business performance.*

8.1   Accounting ratios

Accounting ratios are used by the managers of the business as a decision-making tool and to help in financial interpretation and planning. They may also be used by outsiders who are interested in the performance of the business or who have an interest in the business.

Ratios are also used to predict trends, to compare with other businesses, and can be used by future investors when deciding whether or not to invest.

There are three types of ratio that we are concerned with:

- **Profitability**

- **Liquidity**

- **Efficiency**

They can be used to compare different years for the same business, with similar businesses of the same size in the same sector or comparison with averages for a particular business sector. This process is often referred to as **ratio analysis**.

Ratio analysis may also be used by another business or individual planning a takeover. It may also prove to be a useful tool in the forecasting or budgeting process.

Profitability ratios

- *Gross profit* as a percentage of *sales*

- *Gross profit* as a percentage of *cost of goods sold*

- *Net profit* as a percentage of *sales*

Gross profit as a percentage of sales

This ratio is used to calculate the gross profit as a percentage of sales turnover. Where the percentage is high, it may indicate that the business has a prudent buying policy.

Changes in the ratio can be caused by:

- an increase or a decrease in the selling price (usually a deliberate company policy), or;

- a change in the cost of goods sold (usually outwith the company's control).

The formula used is:

> (gross profit ÷ sales) × 100

Gross profit as a percentage of cost of goods sold

This ratio is used to calculate the gross profit as a percentage of cost of goods sold. Where the percentage is high, it may indicate that the business has a prudent buying policy.

Changes in the ratio can be caused by an increase or a decrease in the cost of goods sold (usually outwith the company's control).

The formula used is:

> (gross profit ÷ cost of goods sold) × 100

Net profit as a percentage of sales

This ratio is used to calculate the return on sales when compared to the total costs of the business. Where a low figure is calculated, this shows that the company's expenses may be high and should be further investigated. This ratio is often used to highlight efficiency and control of costs.

The formula used is:

> (net profit ÷ sales) × 100

Accounting ratios

Q1: Using the values provided complete the ratios in the table.

Go online

	Year 1 £	Year 2 £
Sales	200000	250000
Cost of goods sold	120000	135000
Gross profit	80000	85000
Expenses	20000	25000
Net profit	60000	60000

	Year 1 fraction	Year 1 %	Year 2 fraction	Year 2 %
Gross % as a % of sales				
Gross profit as a % of cost of goods sold				
Net profit as a % of sales				

. . . .

Q2: The gross profit to sales ratio has improved from year 1 to year 2.

a) True
b) False

. . . .

Q3: The gross profit to sales ratio can change after a change in the cost of purchases.

a) True
b) False

. . . .

Q4: A change in the selling price will not change the gross profit ratio.

a) True
b) False

. . . .

Q5: The gross profit to cost of goods sold is worse in Year 2.

a) True
b) False

. . . .

Q6: This means that the cost of goods sold has fallen.

a) True
b) False

. . . .

Q7: The net profit to sales ratio is better in Year 1.

a) True
b) False

. . . .

Q8: The cost of goods sold will affect the net profit ratio.

a) True
b) False

. . . .

Q9: The profitability of this business has improved in Year 2.

a) True
b) False

. . . .

Q10: Ratios can also be used to compare businesses operating in different sectors.

a) True
b) False

. . . .

Q11: Ratios should not be used as a decision-making tool.

a) True
b) False

. . . .

8.2 Liquidity ratios

Liquidity ratios are either **current ratios** or **acid test ratios**.

Current ratio

The current ratio is used to show the business's ability to meet its short-term debts without having to borrow money. There is no ideal figure for this ratio although it should normally fall within the region of 1:1 and 3:1.

- Where the ratio is very low, this indicates that the business may have liquidity problems.

- Where the ratio is high this indicates that there is more than enough money to cover short term business debts, however, it can also indicate that there is too much cash in the business not being used to best advantage. Spare cash can be invested, even in the short term, and earn additional income for the business.

The formula used is:

> current ratio = current assets ÷ current liabilities

Acid test ratio

The acid test ratio is similar to the current ratio although it takes into account the fact that stocks of raw materials and goods for resale can often take some time to be turned into cash.

The business's ability to pay its short-term debts is therefore looked at without including stock.

The average figure of 1:1 should be used as a guideline although anything less than this would show that the business may not be able to meet its short term debts without selling stock or borrowing money.

However, some types of businesses can operate with an acid test ratio of less than 1:1 so the typical ratio will depend on the type of business.

The formula used is:

> acid test ratio = (current assets - stock) ÷ current liabilities

Go online

Current and acid test ratios

Q12: For each company, using the information provided, calculate:

1. Current ratio (current ratio = current assets ÷ current liabilities)
2. Acid test ratio (Acid test ratio = (current assets - stock) ÷ current liabilities

Company	Alpha Ltd £	Beta £
Current assets	45000	46000
Current liabilities	30000	23000
Stock	16000	20000

. . . .

Current and acid test ratios 2

You are the accountant for a business that has been asked to supply both these businesses.

Write a short report (about 150 words) on whether or not you should accept these businesses as customers.

The report should focus on their ability to pay the money they owe your business if you accept them as customers.

Submit your report to your teacher for marking.

. . . .

8.3   Efficiency ratios

Return on capital employed

This ratio measures how well, or how badly, a business has utilised the capital that has been invested in it. This gives a more useful interpretation of performance than merely looking at the profit figure.

When you invest money in a bank, you will probably pick the one with the best interest rates. The concept is similar here. The owner(s) want to know how much their investment will earn in percentage terms.

One business might return a profit of £50,000 based on capital employed of £100,000, while another may have a profit of £100,000 on an investment of £500,000. Although the second business has a higher profit figure, the first business provides a much better return for each £1 invested.

The formula used is:

> return on capital employed = (net profit ÷ capital employed) × 100

Q13: Using the accounting information shown, calculate the return on capital employed for each of the supermarket chains for both 2014 and 2015.

Company	Year	Net/Operating profit £millions	Capital employed £millions
Sainsbarn plc	2014	533.0	4751.0
Sainsbarn plc	2015	625.0	4848.0
Spender plc	2014	440.5	4565.8
Spender plc	2015	643.8	3080.9
Morris's plc	2014	204.3	993.1
Morris's plc	2015	229.8	1113.7

. . . .

Investment advisor

You are investment advisor and have been asked to produce a short report on which of these businesses would provide the best investment opportunity.

Your report should take account of any possible trends between 2014 and 2015 (which is improving, which is getting worse), and should be around 200 words.

Submit your report to your teacher.

. . . .

Mearns plc ratios

Go online

Q14: Using the information provided calculate the following ratios for the two years.

1. Gross percentage as a percentage of sales
2. Gross profit as a percentage of cost of goods sold
3. Net profit as a percentage of sales
4. Current ratio
5. Acid test ratio
6. Return on capital employed

		20x1		20x2
	£000	£000	£000	£000
Net sales		250		320
Cost of goods sold		180		210
Expenses		20		40
Net profit		50		70
Fixed assets		150		160
Current assets				
Bank	15		8	
Debtors	60		80	
Stock	30		40	
Total	105		128	
Current liabilities	55	50	68	60
Financed by				
Capital employed		150		150
Profit		50		70
Total		200		220

	20x1 ratio	20x1 %	20x2 ratio	20x2 %
Gross % as a % of sales				
Gross profit as a %of cost of goods sold				
Net profit as a % of sales				
Current ratio				
Acid test ratio				
Return on capital employed				

. . . .

8.4 The limitations of ratio analysis

Although useful, ratios should not be used as the only basis for decision-making because:

- The information is historical - always out of date.
- You can only compare very similar business of the same size.
- Different businesses can calculate their ratios in different ways.
- The external environment of the business changes from year to year.
- They do not take account of changes within the business such as new machinery.

8.5 Summary questions

Summary questions

Q15: Gross Profit Percentage in interested in a business's liquidity.

Go online

a) True
b) False

. . . .

Q16: Ratio analysis can only be used to compare a business performance with previous years.

a) True
b) False

. . . .

Q17: An increase in Net Profit percentage of sales could indicate a business is using a cheaper supplier.

a) True
b) False

. . . .

Q18: Return on Capital employed ratio requires a business to know its opening capital.

a) True
b) False

. . . .

Q19: Acid test ratio is better than current ratio for showing a business its ability to pay short term debts.

a) True
b) False

. . . .

Q20: Ratio analysis can also highlight issues with staff morale and turnover.

a) True
b) False

. . . .

Q21: Mark up ratio information comes from a business's statement of financial position.

a) True
b) False

. . . .

Q22: Potential investors are mostly interested in a business's Return on Capital Employed.

a) True
b) False

. . . .

Q23: PESTEC is just as important to a business's success as ratio analysis.

a) True
b) False

. . . .

Q24: Efficiency ratios show a business's ability to pay it's short term debts.

a) True
b) False

. . . .

8.6   End of topic tests

End of topic 8 test

Go online

Q25: Which of the following would improve the Gross Profit to Sales Ratio? Choose all that apply.

a) Increasing the selling price.
b) Offering a 10% off sale to customers.
c) Finding a cheaper supplier.
d) Reducing expenses.

. . . .

Q26: Which of the following would change the Gross Profit to Cost of Goods Sold Ratio? Choose all that apply.

a) Decreasing the selling price.

b) Finding a cheaper supplier.

c) Reducing the bank overdraft.

d) Obtaining a discount from the supplier.

. . . .

Q27: Which of the following would change the Net Profit Ratio? Choose all that apply.

a) Finding a cheaper mortgage.

b) Increased investment by the owner(s).

c) Obtaining a loan from the bank.

d) Making an office worker redundant.

. . . .

Q28: Which of the following could change the Acid Test Ratio for a business? Choose all that apply.

a) Increasing the level of stocks.

b) Offering debtors a discount for quick payment.

c) Arranging a bank overdraft.

d) An increase in cash sales.

. . . .

Q29: Which of the following would improve the Return on Capital Employed? Choose all that apply.

a) A reduction in the expenses of the business.

b) An increase in the cost of purchases.

c) An increase in the dividend paid to shareholders.

d) An increase in wages paid to employees.

. . . .

SQA style questions

Q30: Describe accounting ratios managers could use. (4 Marks)

Go online

. . . .

Q31: Explain the limitations of using ratio analysis. (5 Marks)

. . . .

Topic 9

Technology

Contents

Learning objectives

After studying this topic, you should be able to:

- *justify uses of technology in human resource management and financial management;*

- *describe the costs of benefits of using technology.*

9.1 Revision

In the previous topic, we looked at how Marketing and Operations departments use technology to enhance their work. This topic will concentrate on the use of ICT in Finance and Human Resources. But first, recap your knowledge by completing the following exercise.

Use of technology - revision

Match the hardware/software (1-12) with the definition (a-l).

Go online

Q1:

1. Laptop
2. PC
3. Tablet
4. Webcam
5. Mainframe
6. Network
7. Word processing
8. Spreadsheet
9. Database
10. Publisher
11. Email
12. World Wide Web

a) Used to join computers and servers together.
b) Camera that lets you see others during meetings.
c) A small computer, perfect for someone on the go.
d) Used to send messages to many people at once.
e) Used to store data about customers, employees and suppliers.
f) Traditional, desktop computer.
g) Used to calculate annual statements.
h) Large computer, used to store data for the whole organisation.
i) Used to create newsletters and flyers.
j) Used to buy and sell online.
k) Portable computer, with built in camera and touch screen.
l) Used to create reports and letters.

. . . .

9.2   ICT in Human Resources

We have already learned about the work carried out by the Human Resources team. The work they do is enhanced by the use of ICT. For example, advancements in flexible working practices would not have happened without the use of technology. Employees working from home require access to email to allow them to communicate with team mates, suppliers and customers. Meetings can take place from employees home with the use of video conferencing. This means employees do not need to travel to conduct a meeting. Using a PC/laptop and a webcam, video conferencing software allows people to conduct face-to-face meetings using audio and video feeds. E-diaries also benefit employees in the HR department. Interviews, training events and grievance procedures are often conducted by 2 or more employees. E-diaries allow for easier planning of these meetings.

ICT is used extensively during the recruitment and selection process. Word processing software is used to draw up Job Descriptions and Person Specifications as they can be professionally laid out and edited each time a new vacancy comes up. These documents can be posted to prospective candidates, although today most businesses chose to post them online instead. A business can chose to post to their own website or use a dedicated recruitment website.

Search for vacancy

Visit http://www.s1jobs.com/ and search for a vacancy you would be interested in applying to in the future. Try and find a vacancy with a downloadable job description or person specification. Download the files and save them to your own folder.

....

Application forms are then received by the business. Again, these can be word processed or completed online. Go back to the job you found in the previous task. Start the application process to see how the business is wanting to hear from applicants (although don't actually apply!)

Once appointed, a business will want to train its workforce. Online training options give businesses more flexibility. They are expensive to create, but can be accessed via training providers. As they are online, they can be updated regularly and accessed at a time and place of the business's choosing. If you are reading this online then you are using a VLE - SCHOLAR is a great example of online learning - you are working through the content, testing yourself as you go, and your teacher/lecturer can check on your progress too. See Topic 2 - Training - VLE for more information about VLEs.

The HR department is also responsible for keeping up to date with Government legislation. All legislation, from the Scottish Parliament in Holyrood, UK Government in Westminster and the European Parliament in Brussels is held online for businesses to access. Businesses using technology to hold data about customers, suppliers and employees must ensure they comply with specific data protection legislation.

9.3   Legislation

The Data Protection Act 1998 aims to protect the rights of the individual by providing legislation to govern the collection, storage and use of information that is held in electronic or paper file systems.

The Data Protection Registrar holds a list of businesses that are registered under the Data Protection Act and it is the responsibility of the individual business to register their interest with the Registrar. This means that if you are running a business and you hold information on third parties, it is your responsibility to register your business under the Act and follow the rules of the law.

There are eight basic Data Protection Principles which all organisations holding personal data must follow:

1. Obtain and process data fairly and lawfully

2. Register the purpose for which the information is held

3. Not disclose the information in any way that is different from those purposes

4. Only hold information that is adequate, relevant and not excessive for the purposes they require

5. Only hold accurate information and keep it up-to-date where necessary

6. Not hold the information any longer than necessary

7. Take appropriate security measures to keep the information safe

8. Give individuals copies of the information held about themselves if they request it and, where appropriate, correct or erase the information

The Data Protection Principles apply to organisations in both the public and private sectors and also information held about children.

The main job of the Data Protection Registrar is to oversee the enforcement and application of the rules of the Act. The Registrar has the authority to have inaccurate records corrected and erased. The Registrar also deals with complaints by members of the public. A complaint may be raised by an individual where there is a failure to allow access to records or where there has been a breach of one of the data protection principles.

In cases where there has been a serious breach, the individual concerned may be entitled to compensation if it can be successfully proven that they have suffered a loss or damage as a direct result of incorrect information being held by the organisation.

The Data Protection Register is a list of all companies who are registered with the Data Protection Registrar. More information is available at:

http://www.ico.gov.uk/what_we_cover/promoting_data_privacy/keeping_the_register.aspx

The information that appears on the register includes:

- The name of the organisation
- The type of information it holds
- The type of individuals that the organisation hold information about
- What the information is used for
- Where the information was obtained from
- Any other party that the information has been disclosed to
- The name and address of the person that individual should write to if they wish to obtain information

Find out more information about data protection at:

http://www.ico.gov.uk/for_organisations/data_protection/the_guide.aspx

The Computer Misuse Act was passed in 1990 and is of importance to business and individuals alike.

It created three new offences:

- Unauthorised access to computer material
- Unauthorised access with intent to commit or facilitate commission of further offences
- Unauthorised modification of computer material.

It is generally accepted as good business practice nowadays to issue IT Guidelines to all employees. This document should make reference to the provisions of the Computer Misuse Act 1990.

The Freedom of Information Act 2000 is "challenged with the task of reversing the working premise that everything is secret, unless otherwise stated, to a position where everything is public unless it falls into specified excepted cases" (Lord Chancellor's first Annual Report on the implementation of the Freedom of Information Act 2000; November 2001). The Freedom of Information (Scotland) Act 2002 gives everyone two specific separate rights:

- the right to know whether information exists,
- the right to access that information (subject to exemptions).

The individual right of access was introduced on 1 January 2005. The main features of this are:

1. Every written request for information including emails will be considered to be an access request under the Freedom of Information Act. There is no set format, nor is there any requirement to justify the request. There are no citizenship or residency restrictions and the only requirement is that applicants provide a name and address.

2. Access requests must be dealt with within 20 working days.

3. If the information is not available or the information is not supplied the applicant must be told why.

4. In cases where either the precise information covered by the request is unclear or where the scope is so wide as to make it likely that the request would be refused on the grounds of cost, public bodies are encouraged to discuss with the applicant the nature of their request to see whether it can be redefined to lead to a positive outcome.

5. The Act requires public bodies to set up an appeals procedure to review refusals at the request of the applicants, and if the applicant remains unhappy at the refusal there is an avenue of recourse to the Information Commissioner.

To date, the Act has mostly been used by those in the media wishing to find out information about companies and public bodies.

9.4   ICT in Finance

We have previously learned about the work carried out by the Finance department. They also rely heavily on the use of ICT. Budgets and financial statements are often produced using accounting software or a spreadsheet package. This means that changes can be made to the budget very easily and the effects of these changes will be automatically updated in the rest of the budget. Formula can be added to reduce the possibility of errors and what if scenario functions can be added to make future predictions.

The finance department are responsible for the payment of wages to employees. Most businesses will use specialised accounting software to fulfil this role.

Brown Manufacturing Ltd

The following information has been taken from the sales, production, and human resources budget of Brown Manufacturing Ltd.

Go online

	January £	February £	March £	April £	May £
Sales	55,000	49,000	59,000	46,000	60,000
Purchases	22,000	26,000	23,000	30,000	24,000
Wages	4,800	4,600	5,000	44,000	5,100
Warehouse	1,200	1,400	1,200	1,500	1,200
Marketing	1,500	1,500	1,500	1,500	1,500

Copy out the following table and complete the cash budget with this information. You can use any available software package or Microsoft Excel spreadsheet to carry out the task.

Cash budget of Brown Manufacturing Ltd

	January £	February £	March £	April £	May £
Opening balance	25,000				
Cash in					
Sales					
Total cash in					
Cash out					
Purchases					
Wages					
Warehouse					
Marketing					
Administration expenses	1200	1200	1200	1200	1200
Distribution expenses	3000	3000	3000	3000	3000
Power	800	800	800	800	800
Total cash out					
Closing balance					

When you have finished you can compare your answer with the one given.

Write a short report on your observations of the information contained in the budget. Describe any problems and comment on any actions the business should take.

Show this report to your teacher.

. . . .

9.5   Payment of wages and salaries

Wages and salaries are not normally paid in cash to staff although some businesses do still operate on this basis. Most businesses will use a system called Bank Automated Credit System (BACS) to electronically transfer wages and salaries directly to employees' bank accounts. There are several advantages in using this service:

- No need for large sums of money to be kept on the business premises;

- No need for large sums of money to be transported to the business premises;

- Cheaper for the business.

An example pay slip is shown below. You can see it consists of information about the employee, then about his pay and deductions, giving the net pay, which will be paid into the bank with details as shown.

Company name	Employee pay reference	Employee name
Heriot-Watt University	012345	Prof. Plum
Pay and allowances	**Deductions**	**Payment date**
Salary: £ 1655.75	Nat. Ins: £ 157.00	31 Mar 2014
Fees: £ 200.00	Tax: £426.65	
Total pay	**Total deductions**	**Net pay**
£ 1855.75	£ 583.65	£ 1272.10
Pay method	**Bank sort code**	**Account number**
BACS	88 - 66 - 55	7654321

All companies are required to maintain financial records. They are an essential part of the business as they show the history of all the business's activities and provide the basis for internal control, internal reporting, and external reporting to agencies such as the HM revenue and customs.

The HM revenue and customs requires that businesses retain financial records and related documents for a period of 6 years for the purpose of possible investigation. It is an offence not to do this.

Limited companies are required to keep records under the Companies Acts of 2006 and 1989 where it states that it is an offence not to maintain proper financial records.

These records form the basis of many business decisions and without proper financial records, managers would not make correct decisions and the business would not be able to operate effectively or efficiently. Using databases to store this data means the information can be kept securely. Errors can easily be rectified and it is easy to delete the data after the 6 year time frame has lapsed.

Direct credit services

Visit http://www.bacs.co.uk and then write a short report on direct credit services.
The report should be around 200 words.

Submit the completed report to your teacher.

. . . .

9.6 Costs and benefits of using ICT

The use of ICT gives both costs and benefits. Like most business costs, organisations
are happy to bear the costs where they can demonstrate that the benefits outweigh the
costs.

Costs of using IT:

- Initial and on-going costs of hardware and equipment.
- On-going costs of replacing and upgrading systems.
- New furniture to house equipment.
- Staff training - leading to a loss of working time.
- Losses in efficiency as even staff who have been trained to use the new system
  will be unfamiliar with it for a period of time and more likely to make mistakes.
- Teething problems will also contribute to inefficiencies.
- Computer viruses/hacking.
- Health and safety issues for staff e.g. repetitive strain injury, backache, eyestrain.

Benefits of using IT:

- Increased efficiency.
- Increased flexibility.
- Increase in the amount of data and information that can be handled.
- Increased customer satisfaction.
- Competitive edge until rivals catch up.
- Possibility of reduced staffing costs.
- Creation of home workers.
- Access to new markets and customers.

Go online

Costs and benefits of using ICT

Q2: Complete the paragraph using following words.

word processing	email	website	databases
spreadsheet	internet	webcam	video conferencing

Employees working from home require access to _____ to allow them to communicate with team mates, suppliers and customers. Meetings can take place from employees home with the use of _____ . Using a PC/laptop and a _____ , video conferencing software allows people to conduct face-to-face meetings using audio and video feeds. ICT is used extensively during the recruitment and selection process. _____ software is used to draw up Job Descriptions and Person Specifications. A business can chose to post vacancies to their own website or use a dedicated recruitment _____ . Once appointed, a business will want to train its workforce. Online training using the _____ give businesses more flexibility. They are expensive to create, but can be accessed via training providers. Budgets and financial statements are often produced using accounting software or a _____ package. This means that changes can be made to the budget very easily. Businesses can use _____ to store data securely. This software allows them to sort and filter the data.

. . . .

9.7   Summary questions

Summary questions

Q3: Meetings using webcams is called Video Conferencing.

Go online

a) True
b) False

....

Q4: E-diaries allow colleagues to view each others appointments.

a) True
b) False

....

Q5: Intranets are used to post external job vacancies.

a) True
b) False

....

Q6: The main benefit of using databases is the ability to produce calculations using formula.

a) True
b) False

....

Q7: The most common way to pay wages and salaries is called BICS.

a) True
b) False

....

Q8: All limited companies are required to produce and maintain financial records.

a) True
b) False

....

Q9: Online training provides feedback to employers.

a) True
b) False

....

Q10: The HM revenue and customs requires that businesses retain financial documents for a period of 8 years.

a) True
b) False

....

9.8   End of topic tests

End of topic 9 test

Go online

Q11: Match the task (1-7) with the application (a-g).

1. Details of new training programmes must be seen by all employees.
2. Departmental budgets must be analysed.
3. Financial summaries must be sent to every director electronically.
4. New legislation has been introduced - A5 postcards need to be made up.
5. A PLC needs to allow all shareholders, and prospective shareholders, to see a summary of their financial performance.
6. Letters need to be produced to inform all shareholders of the upcoming AGM.
7. All suppliers' contact details must be stored safely and securely.

a) Spreadsheet
b) Internet
c) Intranet
d) Database
e) Email
f) Desktop Publishing
g) Word Processing

....

Q12: Complete the paragraphs using following words.

competent	flexibility	upgrading	strain	competitive
satisfaction	hardware	hackers	efficiency	

Initial and on-going costs of _____ and equipment can be expensive for business. They also must deal with the on-going costs of replacing and _____ systems. Staff also need to be trained to ensure they are _____ in using the machinery. This can lead to a loss of working time. ICT programs may be susceptible to computer viruses or _____ , which are people who intentionally try and steal or corrupt your data. Staff may also feel the impact of continually working at a computer, with symptoms such as repetitive _____ injury, backache or eyestrain. A business can use ICT to complete tasks more quickly, which leads to increased _____ . Edits can also be made, leading to greater _____ . Sending out standardised information leads to increased customer _____ . Streamlining processes can also lead to a _____ edge until rivals catch up.

....

SQA style questions

Go online

Q13: Explain the benefits to an organisation of introducing ICT. (3 Marks)

....

Q14: Explain the benefits of using ICT for the Human Resources department. (3 Marks)

....

Topic 10

End of unit tests

End of unit 3 test

Go online

Identify whether the following procedures belong to the recruitment or selection process.

Q1: Holding panel interviews

a) Selection
b) Recruitment

....

Q2: Drawing a person specification

a) Selection
b) Recruitment

....

Q3: Advertising internally

a) Selection
b) Recruitment

....

Q4: Receiving application forms

a) Selection
b) Recruitment

....

Decide true or false for the following statements.

Q5: Empowerment is when employees are given the power to make certain decisions without consulting the manager each time.

a) True
b) Flase

....

Q6: Quality Oval is a group of workers who come together with management to discuss an issue or how to improve a situation.

a) True
b) Flase

....

Q7: Return to work interviews are mandatory after each period of absence.

a) True
b) Flase

....

Q8: Trade union/professional association membership will ensure employees feel they have a channel to voice their opinions.

a) True
b) Flase

. . . .

Q9: Harassment is included as part of the Equality Act 2010.

a) True
b) Flase

. . . .

Select the correct source of finance for each definition.

Q10: Obtain a loan an individual who will receive a share in the organisation in return.

a) Bank loan
b) Commercial mortgage
c) Venture capitalists

. . . .

Q11: A sum of money paid back with interest.

a) Bank loan
b) Commercial mortgage
c) Venture capitalists

. . . .

Q12: A loan secured against property owned by the organisation.

a) Bank loan
b) Commercial mortgage
c) Venture capitalists

. . . .

Match the theory (1-3) with the theorist (a-c).

Q13:

1. Hierarchy of needs
2. Theory X and Y
3. Hygiene and motivators

a) Douglas McGregor
b) Abraham Maslow
c) Frederick Herzberg

. . . .

Complete the descriptions using following terms.

- Virtual

- Off-the-job

- On-the-job

- Work-based

- Induction

Q14: _____ training course are developed and led by staff within an organisation. They can include a mixture of on-the-job and off-the-job initiatives.

. . . .

Q15: _____ training takes place when an employee is not doing the job. This can involve a workshop with an in-house trainer or attending an external training course.

. . . .

Q16: _____ training takes place whilst the employees is doing their job. This can involve being coached by a more experienced colleague.

. . . .

Q17: _____ training is used for new staff and includes information such as the organisations layout and health and safety requirements.

. . . .

Q18: _____ training involves making use of online resources and discussion forums to up-skill or explore ideas with colleagues and other professionals.

. . . .

Match the terms (1-6) with the definitions (a-f).

Q19:

1. Cash flow
2. Drawings
3. Debtor
4. Creditor
5. Expenses
6. Capital

a) Money owed to the business.
b) Money paid out of the business for items such as rent, electricity and wages.

c) Money withdrawn from the business by the owner for their personal use.

d) Someone the business owes money to.

e) The money invested by the owner or owners of the business to set it up.

f) The movement of cash in and out of a business.

....

Decide true or false for the following statements.

Q20: Trading account shows the profit and loss made from buying and selling stock over a period of time.

a) True

b) False

....

Q21: Income statement shows the overall profit or loss at a specific moment in time.

a) True

b) False

....

Q22: Statement of financial position shows the financial position of a business over the past year.

a) True

b) False

....

Q23: Cash budgets show projected income and expenditure for the following year.

a) True

b) False

....

SQA style questions

Q24: Describe the external sources of recruitment available to an HR manager. (5 Marks)

Go online

....

Q25: Discuss the costs and benefits of training staff. (8 Marks)

....

Q26: Describe the advantages and disadvantages of different styles of leadership. (6 Marks)

....

Q27: Describe the importance of maintaining positive employee relations. (4 Marks)

....

Q28: Other than the Equality Act 2010, describe **two** pieces of legislation affecting organisations. (4 Marks)

....

Q29: Describe possible sources of finance for a PLC looking to expand its activities. (4 Marks)

....

Q30: Describe the purpose of a cash budget. (3 Marks)

....

Q31: Explain the usefulness of a statement of financial position and of a profit and income statement. (2 Marks)

....

Q32: Outline **four** accounting ratios. (4 Marks)

....

Q33: Justify the use of a spreadsheet in the finance department. (4 Marks)

....

Glossary

"Off-the-job" training

training that takes place instead of the employee completing their work, at the employees workplace or at a training provider.

Acid test ratio

shows a business's ability to pay its short term debts but with stock removed from the calculation.

Advisory

to give impartial advice on a number of matters.

Application form

a series of questions designed to demonstrate the knowledge and experience of a prospective candidate.

Appraisal

a one-to-one evaluation of an employees' achievements and development needs.

Aptitude test

an assessment, usually completed online, designed to show how competent a candidate is in a certain skill, such as driving, or language.

Arbitration

is where an impartial person makes a decision on a dispute.

Asset

items that the business owns.

Autocratic

a leader who does not believe in giving responsibility to others.

Capital

the money invested by the owner or owners of the business to set it up.

Carriage inwards

the cost of transporting or delivering stocks purchased by the business.

Cash flow

the movement of cash in and out of a business.

Cash inflow

movement of cash into the business.

Cash outflow

movement of cash out of the business.

Closing stock

the value of unsold stock at the end of the financial period.

Collective bargaining

a group, normally a trade union, who speak for a large number of people.

Conciliation

an attempt to bring together two parties who are at odds.

Corporation tax

a tax on business profits payable to the Government.

Cost of sales

the cost to the business of the products that it has sold.

Counselling

trained staff who give support and advice to employees in need.

Creditor

an individual or business whom you owe money to.

Current assets

cash, or assets, that can be turned into cash in the near future such as stock and debtors.

Current liabilities

money that the business has to pay out in the near future- such as creditors and bank overdraft. Normally defined as having to be paid in less than a year's time.

Current ratio

shows a business's ability to pay its short term debts.

Debentures

a group of loans that pays monthly interest and the full loan at the end of the term.

Debt factor

selling your debt to another business.

Debtor

an individual or business who owes you money.

Democratic

a leader who believes in involving others in the decision making.

Dividend

proportion of the business profit paid to shareholders and for each share they own.

Drawings

money withdrawn from the business by the owner for their personal use.

Efficiency

ratios used to show how a business is performing and the returns it is generating.

E-learning

training that takes place online using either a training provider or professional learning communities on social media.

Employee relations

the way employers deal with and interact with their employees as individuals or as a group.

Esteem factors

Maslow's belief in making the employee feel valued and recognising their job title and place within the business.

Expenses

money paid out of the business for items such as rent, electricity and wages.

Fixed assets

things that the business owns and intends to keep for more than a year. They can be used to generate profit. For example, premises and machinery.

Flexi-time

employees may be required to work within essential periods but outside 'core times' they often get flexibility in how they work their hours.

Grievance

a statement of complaint over something believed to be wrong or unfair.

Gross profit

the money a business makes before expenses have been paid.

Gross profit percentage

the percentage of sales that a business has turned into gross profit.

HM revenue and customs

the Government department responsible for collecting taxes from UK businesses and employees.

Home working

new technology makes communication with office and customers possible by telephone, fax and email from home.

Hygiene factors

Herzberg's belief that employees are demotivated if they do not receive material benefits or a good working relationship.

Income statement

shows a summary of the business's trading activity during the financial year.

Induction training

basic training for new employees.

Intranet

an internal Internet allowing only people within the business to view it.

Job analysis

a brief document outlining a vacancy that requires to be filled.

Job description

a document outlining the purpose of the job, the hours to be worked, the tasks involved and who the individual would report to and be responsible for.

Job-sharing

two employees share the work normally done by one employee.

Laissez-faire

a leadership style where subordinates are given the freedom to make their own decision.

Legislation

an act of parliament that sets out rules and regulations that must be adhered to.

Liabilities

monies owed.

Liquidity

the ability of a business to generate enough cash to meet its bills and other short-term financial obligations as they become due.

Long-term liabilities

debts of the business that are not due to be repaid for more than 12 months. For example bank loans, debentures, and mortgages.

Mark-up ratio

measures how much profit has been added to the selling price of a good.

Motivation

an incentive to do better.

Net profit

the money a business makes after expenses have been paid.

Net profit percentage

the percentage of sales that a business has turned into net profit.

Net worth

the amount the business is worth; calculated by adding opening capital and net profit.

Opening stock of goods

the value of the stock at the start of the financial period.

Overdraft

bank allows you to withdraw more money than you have in your account.

Part-time working

an employee who does not work full time hours, for example 4 days a week, or mornings only.

Person specification

a document outlining the skills, qualities and experience needed of the individual seeking employment.

Physiological factors

Maslow's belief in the basic needs that the employee will satisfy through the receiving wages.

Profitability

ratios used to show how profitable a business is compared to previous or competitor performance.

Psychometric tests

an assessment, usually completed online, designed to show the personality, attitudes and character of the applicant.

Purchase returns

the value of stock purchased but returned to the supplier due to defects.

Purchases

the cost of stocks that the business has bought.

Reserves

money and profits that are retained in the business and not paid out to the owners. It can be for a specific purpose such as planned expansion.

Retained profit

money that a business makes and keeps for use in the future.

Return on capital employed

measures the expected return to be paid on an investment into the business.

Safety factors

Maslow's belief in offering permanent contracts to encourage the feeling of security.

Sales

money that the business has received from selling goods and/or services.

Sales revenue

the money generated from selling stock.

Self-actualisation factors

Maslow's belief in allowing the employee to make their own independent decisions and goals.

Share issue

limited companies sell a percentage of their business in return for an investment.

Shift-working

widespread in industries, which must run on a 24-hour cycle, such as newspaper production, utilities and hospital and emergency services.

Social factors

Maslow's belief in encouraging team work and job rotation; allowing employees to learn from and encourage one another.

Staff development

the total skills and qualifications gained by an employee taking part in training opportunities.

Staggered hours

employees in the same workplace have different start, finish and break times - often as a way of covering longer opening hours.

Teleworking

working from your car or other remote locations.

Term-time working

an employee on a permanent contract takes paid or unpaid leave during school holidays.

Theory X

a motivation theory that assumes workers are lazy and only interested in money.

Theory Y

a motivation theory that assumes workers are interested in job satisfaction and achieving objectives.

Trade credit

buying purchases and paying later.

Trade union

a body that is formed to represent a workforce.

True motivators

Hertzberg's belief that employees are motivated by the opportunity of advancement and job satisfaction.

Turnover/net sales

the value of the business's sales less any returns.

Unappropriated profit

profit retained in the business, i.e. not distributed to either owners or shareholders.

Venture capitalist

an individual or business that invests in a riskier business for a higher return on their investment.

Work based training

a long term approach where an employee is trained by the organisation.

Workforce planning

ensuring you have the right people, with the right skills, at the right time.

Working capital or Net current assets

this is the difference between the total current assets and the total current liabilities.

Answers to questions and activities

1 Recruitment and selection

Flexible working patterns (page 3)

Q1:   1c; 2e; 3g; 4d; 5a; 6h; 7f; 8b

Answers from page 4.

Q2:

- To decide what tasks they want the post holder to perform.
- It can be used as the basis for an advertisement of the vacancy.
- It will let any applicants decide if they want the job.

Q3:

- The job title.
- Who is accountable for the employee.
- Who is accountable to the employee.
- The location of the job.
- A brief description of what the job entails.
- A list of duties and responsibilities.
- Hours of work.
- Working conditions and pay.

Recruitment process - descriptions (page 5)

Q4:   The purpose of a **job analysis** is to find out whether a vacancy exists and what the job will be.

Q5:   The purpose of a **job description** is to identify what tasks the organisation wants the post holder to perform.

Q6:   The purpose of a **person specification** is to identify the individual that you want to do the job.

Sources of recruitment (page 7)

Q7:   Internal

Q8:   External

Q9:   Internal

Q10: External

Q11: External

Q12: External

Q13: Internal

Q14: External

Q15: Internal

Q16: Internal

Answers from page 9.

Q17: c) all applicants answer the same questions.

Q18: a) the person specification.

Q19: c) The most suitable applicants will be invited for interview.

Q20: c) the job description.

Q21: b) attract a number of suitable candidates.

Types of selection methods (page 11)

Q22: 1f; 2a; 3e; 4b; 5d; 6c

Summary questions (page 12)

Q23: b) False

Q24: a) True

Q25: a) True

Q26: b) False

Q27: b) False

Q28: a) True

Q29: a) True

Q30: b) False

Q31: b) False

Q32: a) True

End of topic 1 test (page 13)

Q33: 1d; 2j; 3a; 4h; 5f; 6b; 7e; 8c; 9i; 10g

Q34: 1c; 2g; 3e; 4j; 5a; 6d; 7k; 8h; 9l; 10i; 11b; 12f

SQA style questions (page 14)

Q35:

- Allows candidates from outside the organisation to bring in new ideas.
- Can target prospective candidates nationally.
- Can use specialist sources such as the TES for specialist posts.
- Job centre or recruitment agencies can do a lot of the background work and send only properly qualified candidates.
- Can be useful to fill vacancies quickly.
- Reduces recruitment costs for organisations.
- The use of external sources can be more expensive than internal.
- Can mean candidates require thorough testing/interviews to assess knowledge and skills base.
- Avoids jealousy from rival internal candidates.

Q36:

- Flexi-time - whereby employees can vary their start and finish times.
- Job share - 2 employees share one full-time job.
- Teleworking - where employees can work away from the office using telecommunications to keep in touch with the office.
- Hot-desking - is an arrangement whereby workers, who work outwith the office, do not have their own desks but work space can be booked according to their needs.
- Career break: is an extended period of leave from work - the intention is that the employee will return to work at the end of the agreed period - eg a year taken to pursue a further qualification.
- Condensed working hours - an arrangement whereby full-time hours are packed into 4 days a week by working longer hours on these days.
- Home working - when an employee spends some or all of their working week working at home.
- Part-time where a worker works for part of the week, usually mornings/afternoons only or 2 or 3 days.
- Shift work where employees work in times intervals to ensure the workforce is always in production.
- Temporary contract where an employee will be employed on a non-permanent basis.
- Fixed term where the employee has a fixed end date.

Q37: Any five from:

- It allows candidates from outside the organisation to bring in new ideas.
- It can target prospective candidates nationally.
- It can use specialist sources such as the TES for specialist posts.
- Job centre or recruitment agencies can do a lot of the background work and send only properly qualified candidates.

- It can be useful to fill vacancies quickly.
- It reduces recruitment costs for organisations.
- The use of external sources can be more expensive than internal.
- It can mean that candidates require thorough testing/interviews to assess knowledge and skills base.
- It avoids jealousy from rival internal candidates.

2 Training and development

Costs of training (page 20)

Q1:
While they are away training, the **quantity** and **quality** of employees work can fall. **Trained** employees may be able to get a better **job** elsewhere. The staff in the **training** department will be an **additional** cost for the business. **Replacement** staff will have to be brought in while staff are **away** training. Training will cost the business **money**.

Summary questions (page 21)

Q2: a) True

Q3: a) True

Q4: b) False

Q5: a) True

Q6: b) False

End of topic 2 test (page 22)

Q7: 1c; 2e; 3a; 4d; 5b

Q8: **Induction** training is for new members of staff. Its purpose is to give new staff members the best possible start. A business that is fully committed to staff **development** will give employees a variety of training options. This is because they see the value in developing staff, both to increase **productivity** and efficiency, whilst reducing staff **turnover**. **"On-the-job"** training takes place whilst the employee is completing their daily routine. It usually involves being coached or mentored by a colleague. Conversely, **"off-the-job"** training takes place when the employee is not involved in their usual routine. This may take place during a training day organised and managed by the business, or at an event being promoted by an **external** training provider. To save costs and improve efficiency, many large organisations have abandoned the more traditional training providers and are creating their own **internal** work based training schemes. Many others are taking to the Internet to provide **e-learning** opportunities for staff.

SQA style questions (page 22)

Q9:
- Induction training is used for new staff and includes information such as the organisations layout and health and safety requirements.
- "On the job" training takes place whilst the employees is doing their job. This can involve being coached by a more experienced colleague.
- "Off the job" training takes place when an employee is not doing the job. This

can involve a workshop with an in-house trainer or attending an external training course.

- Work-based training course are developed and led by staff within an organisation. They can include a mixture of on-the-job and off-the-job initiatives.

- Virtual training, or e-learning, involves making use of online resources and discussion forums to up-skill or explore ideas with colleagues and other professionals.

Q10: Any four from:

- It allows for a wider pool of skills to be available to the organisation.
- It allows staff to carry out a wider range of tasks.
- It provides cover for absent colleagues.
- It is motivational for staff and will improve performance.
- It can improve the quality of product/service provided.
- It improves customer relations.
- It improves the image of the organisation and they will attract a better calibre of worker.
- It might reduce the number of accidents at work.
- It may be required to introduce change/make the staff more acceptable to change.
- It allows the organisation to be more flexible in the marketplace.

3 Motivation and leadership

Hierarchy of needs (page 25)

Q1:

1. Self - actualisation
2. Esteem
3. Social
4. Safety
5. Physiological

Hierarchy of needs - definitions (page 25)

Q2: Esteem

Q3: Safety

Q4: Physiological

Q5: Self - actualisation

Q6: Social

Douglas McGregor - Theory X and Theory Y (page 26)

Q7:

Theory x	Theory Y
"Money is the only thing that matters to me."	"I enjoy my work as I am given praise when I do well."
"I don't want promotion, who can be bothered with the hassle?"	"I have a sense of pride in my work and everything I have achieved."
"I'm content where I am."	"If I want extra responsibility my boss will find a way to give it to me."

Frederick Herzberg - Hygiene factors and motivators (page 28)

Q8:

Hygiene factors	Motivators
Company policies	Challenging work
Company benefits	Sense of achievement
Supervisors	Recognition
Good wages	A love of the job

Summary questions (page 30)

Q9: b) False

Q10: a) True

Q11: b) False

Q12: a) True

Q13: a) True

End of topic 3 test (page 31)

Q14: 1b: 2c: 3a

Q15: c) Physiological

Q16: b) Self-actualisation

Q17: a) Hygiene factor

Q18: a) True

Q19: b) False

SQA style questions (page 32)

Q20: Any five from:

- Ensure employees have good pay and conditions to keep them satisfied.
- Have a clear career structure and policy of internal recruitment to provide opportunities for promotion.
- Carry out staff appraisals where employees meet with their line manager to discuss their progress within the business.
- Offer permanent contracts so employees feel they have job security.
- Set up a works council where a group of worker representatives and management have joint decision-making powers on employee-related matters.
- Set up quality circles where groups of workers can meet regularly to identify and attempt to solve work-related issues.

Q21: Any two from:

- Elton Mayo: He was focussed on importance of social factors and human behaviour; stressed importance of taking into account workers' needs in order to improve productivity.
- Abraham Maslow: He described hierarchy of needs, broadly satisfied in order; management methods need to be appropriate to the level on which workers are currently operating.

- Frederick Herzberg: He identified hygiene factors (e.g. pay) and motivators (e.g. recognition).
- Douglas McGregor: He came up with Theory X and Theory Y. In Theory X managers viewed workers as inherently lazy and resistant to change; mainly motivated by money. In Theory Y managers viewed workers as motivated; keen to use initiative. Theory Y view is more aligned with HR School, Theory X with classical school.

4 Employee relations

Answers from page 35.

Q1: a) True

Q2: a) True

Q3: b) False

Q4: b) False

Q5: a) True

Q6: b) False

Q7: b) False

Q8: b) False

Q9: a) True

Q10: b) False

Answers from page 38.

Q11: c) at least once a year.

Q12: b) the line manager.

Answers from page 39.

Q13: a) training needs of the employee.

Q14: d) assess the performance of the employee.

Q15: c) both the employee and the line manager.

Employee relations (page 41)

Q16:

The purpose of **negotiation** is to come to an **agreement** between two or more parties. Employers are legally obliged to **consult** their workers about some changes in the workplace. **Arbitration** is used when the parties cannot negotiate an agreement. Employment Tribunals are used by employees who have been allegedly **unfairly** treated by their employer. **Strikes** are where the employees stop working. **Boycotts** are used when the employees do not agree with **changes** in the workplace.

Dell (page 43)

Q17: a) True

Q18: b) False

Q19: b) False

Q20: b) False

Q21: b) False

Employment law (page 47)

Q22: National Minimum Wage Act 1998

Q23: Equality Act 2010

Q24: Employment Rights Act 1996

Q25: Employment Relations Act 2004

Q26: Working Time Regulations Act 1998

Q27: Employment Act 2002

Health and safety at work (page 48)

Q28:
All staff are **trained** and informed of **potential** dangers. Appoint safety **officers** and committees which will carry out regular **inspection** of the workplace and assess the dangers involved in each job. The employer must make sure that they take every reasonable step to ensure that all machinery is properly **maintained**. All **hazardous** substances are dealt with properly. The employees are expected to behave in a **reasonable** manner at work and must take some responsibility for their own **actions**. Follow all **instructions** and accept **training** where appropriate.

Summary questions (page 49)

Q29: b) False

Q30: a) True

Q31: a) True

Q32: b) False

Q33: a) True

Q34: a) True

Q35: b) False

Q36: b) False

Q37: a) True

Q38: a) True

Q39: a) True

Q40: a) True

Q41: b) False

Q42: a) True

Q43: a) True

End of topic 4 test (page 51)

Q44: Arbitration

Q45: Advisory

Q46: Conciliation

Q47: 1b; 2f; 3a; 4d; 5c; 6e

Q48:

1. Age
2. Disability
3. Gender reassignment
4. Marriage and civil partnership
5. Pregnancy and maternity
6. Race
7. Religion or belief
8. Sex
9. Sexual orientation

SQA style questions (page 52)

Q49: Any four from:

- Good employee relations will help ensure that the organisation meets its objectives.
- Workers are usually much happier and more motivated.
- They are more committed to the goals of the business.
- Workers are more accepting of change and more flexible in their response to requests.
- They are more able to recognise the need for the organisation to achieve its objectives.

Q50: Any four from:

- The terms and conditions of employment for staff.

- Procedures for dealing with staff complaints (grievance).
- The procedures for disciplining of staff.
- Redundancy - including any agreed payments.
- The involvement of staff in decision-making.
- Trade Union recognition.
- Collective bargaining - discussions with staff on pay and conditions or changes to working practices for all employees.

Q51: Any four from:

- Quality circle is a group of workers who come together with management to discuss an issue or how to improve a situation.
- Works councils are made up of an equal number of employees and managers meeting to discuss issues.
- Open door management policies - managers will meet with employees at any appropriate time.
- Empowerment is when employees are given the power to make certain decisions without consulting the manager each time.
- Appraisal is when staff meet with a line manager to discuss their progress.
- Negotiation when trade union officials and managers meet to agree a suitable course of action.
- Consultation with members to ensure that the views of everyone are heard and listened to.
- Training opportunities will motivate staff as they feel valued.
- Promotion opportunities will motivate employees to want to work harder.
- Trade Union/Professional association membership will ensure employees feel they have a channel to voice their opinions.

Q52: Any four from:

- Managers are required to be aware that new legislation exists.
- Provides protection for employees who have "protected characteristics".
- Organisation cannot discriminate because of:
  - age;
  - disability;
  - gender;
  - pregnancy;
  - maternity.
- Harassment - employees can complain of behaviour they find offensive even if it is not directed at them.
- Victimisation - someone is treated badly because they have made/supported a complaint or grievance under the act.

5 Sources of finance

Sources of finance (page 56)

Q1:

1. Medium-term
2. Short-term
3. Long-term
4. Short-term
5. Short-term
6. Medium-term
7. Long-term
8. Long-term
9. Short-term
10. Medium-term
11. Short-term
12. Long-term

Answers from page 56.

Q2: b) False

Q3: a) True

Q4: b) False

Q5: a) True

Q6: a) True

Q7: a) True

Q8: b) False

Answers from page 58.

Q9: a) True

End of topic 5 test (page 58)

Q10: 1d; 2g; 3h; 4a; 5e; 6b; 7c; 8f

Q11:

Internal	External
Retained profit	Venture capital
Owner's savings	Hire purchase
Share issue	Debentures
	Bank loan
	Bank overdraft
	Leasing
	Debt factoring

Q12: b) Share issue

Q13: c) Leasing

Q14: c) Overdraft

Q15: b) Retained profit

Q16: a) Debentures

SQA style questions (page 60)

Q17:

- Bank loan - a loan paid back with interest.
- Commercial mortgage - a loan secured against property owned by the organisation.
- Sell assets/land - sell unwanted assets to raise funds.
- Venture capitalists - obtain a loan from a venture capitalist who will receive a share in the organisation in return.
- Retained profits - use profits from previous years to fund the takeover.

6 Cash budgeting

Cash budget: Winmill Confectionery (page 65)

Q1: The individual changes outlined will alter the Cash budget as follows:

	Jan	Feb	Mar	Apr	May	Jun
	£	£	£	£	£	£
Opening balance	15400	14300	13800	14900	-2200	-1500
Cash in						
Shop sales	8500	9100	6700	12000	13000	17500
Wholesale	16000	16000	20000	20000	20000	28000
Contract sales	13500	13500	13500	800	14500	14500
Total cash in	38000	38600	40200	32800	47500	60000
Cash out						
Materials	10800	10800	10800	21600	18000	18000
Wages	17500	17500	17500	17500	17500	17500
Rent	1000	1000	1000	1000	1500	1500
Insurance	1200	1200	1200	1200	1200	1200
Telephone	130	130	130	130	130	130
Administration expenses	2300	2300	2300	2300	2300	2300
Distribution expenses	6000	6000	6000	6000	6000	6000
Power	170	170	170	170	170	170
Total cash out	39100	39100	39100	49900	46800	46800
Closing balance	14300	13800	14900	-2200	-1500	11700

	Jan	Feb	Mar	Apr	May	Jun
	£	£	£	£	£	£
Opening balance	15400	13100	10900	10300	-9700	-11750
Cash in						
Shop sales	8500	9100	6700	12000	13000	17500
Wholesale	16000	16000	20000	20000	20000	28000
Contract sales	13500	13500	13500	800	14500	14500
Total cash in	38000	38600	40200	32800	47500	60000
Cash out						
Materials	12000	12000	12000	24000	20000	20000
Wages	17500	17500	17500	17500	17500	17500
Rent	1000	1500	1500	1500	2250	2250
Insurance	1200	1200	1200	1200	1200	1200
Telephone	130	130	130	130	130	130
Administration expenses	2300	2300	2300	2300	2300	2300
Distribution expenses	6000	6000	6000	6000	6000	6000
Power	170	170	170	170	170	170
Total cash out	40300	40800	40800	52800	49550	49550
Closing balance	13100	10900	10300	-9700	-11750	-1300

	Jan £	Feb £	Mar £	Apr £	May £	Jun £
Opening balance	15400	13100	12200	12900	-5800	-6300
Cash in						
Shop sales	8500	9100	6700	12000	13000	17500
Wholesale	16000	16000	20000	20000	20000	28000
Contract sales	13500	14300	14300	1600	15300	15300
Total cash in	38000	39400	41000	33600	48300	60800
Cash out						
Materials	12000	12000	12000	24000	20000	20000
Wages	17500	17500	17500	17500	17500	17500
Rent	1000	1000	1000	1000	1500	1500
Insurance	1200	1200	1200	1200	1200	1200
Telephone	130	130	130	130	130	130
Administration expenses	2300	2300	2300	2300	2300	2300
Distribution expenses	6000	6000	6000	6000	6000	6000
Power	170	170	170	170	170	170
Total cash out	40300	40300	40300	52300	48800	48800
Closing balance	13100	12200	12900	-5800	-6300	5700

	Jan £	Feb £	Mar £	Apr £	May £	Jun £
Opening balance	15400	13100	11400	9550	-11700	-14750
Cash in						
Shop sales	8500	9100	6700	12000	13000	17500
Wholesale	16000	16000	20000	20000	20000	28000
Contract sales	13500	13500	13500	800	14500	14500
Total cash in	38000	38600	40200	32800	47500	60000
Cash out						
Materials	12000	12000	12000	24000	20000	20000
Wages	17500	17500	19250	19250	19250	19250
Rent	1000	1000	1000	1000	1500	1500
Insurance	1200	1200	1200	1200	1200	1200
Telephone	130	130	130	130	130	130
Administration expenses	2300	2300	2300	2300	2300	2300
Distribution expenses	6000	6000	6000	6000	6000	6000
Power	170	170	170	170	170	170
Total cash out	40300	40300	42050	54050	50550	50550
Closing balance	13100	11400	9550	-11700	-14750	-5300

Answers from page 66.

Q2: Possible answers: Insurance, Fuel, Advertising, Car servicing, Car repairs, Cleaning, Licenses.

Answers from page 67.

Q3: b) Sale of a small warehouse.

Q4: a) Building a factory extension.

Summary question (page 68)

Q5: b) False

Q6: a) True

Q7: a) True

Q8: a) True

Q9: b) False

End of topic 6 test (page 69)

Q10: Companies need to **budget** and be aware of cash flow in order to stay solvent. Cash flow is the movement of money in and out of the business. Cash flows out when **expenses** are paid and cash flows into the business when **sales** are made. **Profit** and cash flow are two very different things. Cash flow is simply about money coming and going from the business. The challenge for **managers** is to make sure there is always enough cash to pay expenses when they are due, as running out of cash threatens the survival of the business. A business can improve its cash flow by reducing cash **outflows**, e.g. by delaying the payment of bills, securing better trade credit terms or factoring. Increasing cash inflows can happen by chasing **debtors**, selling assets or securing **an overdraft**.

SQA style questions (page 69)

Q11: Any four from:

- Too much money tied up in stock.
- Customers being given too long a credit period.
- Customers being given too high a credit limit.
- Owners taking out too much money through drawings.
- Having high borrowing with increased rates of interest.
- Suppliers not allowing credit or very short credit period.
- Sales revenue is not high enough.
- Sudden increase in expenses.

- Capital expenditure is too high.

Q12: Any four from:

- It makes department managers accountable.
- It allows managers to plan.
- It allows target setting for staff.
- It helps prepare for any shortfall of cash in advance.
- Expenditure can be more tightly controlled.
- It allows remedial action to be taken if things go wrong.
- It allows better use of money if surplus can be predicted.
- Problems can arise if poor planning.
- Staffing and resources have to be taken into account.

7 Financial statements

Coulter: Income statement (page 76)

Q1:

	£	£
turnover		220000
cost of sales		
opening stock of goods	70000	
purchases	85000	
	155000	
less closing stock of goods	60000	95000
gross profit		125000
other operating profit		
rent received	4000	4000
		129000
expenses		
wages	35000	
carriage out	3000	
office expenses	12000	
advertising	4000	
telephone	5000	
heat and light	9000	
bank interest	2000	70000
Net profit		59000

Answers from page 78.

Q2: c) Printing Presses

Q3: d) Stocks of Paper

Q4: b) Payments for Printing Inks

Answers from page 79.

Q5: a) Loans on their premises

Q6: NET WORTH

Lawrenson: Statement of financial position (page 81)

Q7:

	£000	£000	£000
Fixed assets		3300	
premises		300	
machinery		500	
delivery vehicles		200	4300
Current assets			
Debtors	600		
Stocks	400		
Cash at bank	200	1200	
Current liabilities			
Creditors	700		
Ordinary dividends	300		
Tax	100	1100	
Net current assets			100
Total assets less current liabilities			4400
Long-term liabilities			
Bank loan		500	
Debentures (5%)		400	900
Net assets			3500
Capital reserves			
Ordinary share capital		3000	
Retained profits		500	
Net assets			3500

Users of financial information (page 82)

Q8:   1d; 2e; 3b; 4c; 5f; 6a

Summary questions (page 83)

Q9:   c) Fixed assets

Q10: b) Trading account

Q11: c) Expenses

Q12: c) a; d

Q13: b) Turnover

Q14: d) Working capital

Q15: a) a; c

Q16: c) b; c; d

Q17: b) Net Assets and Net Worth

Q18: c) Capital

End of topic 7 test (page 85)

Q19:

Income statement	Statement of financial position
Sales revenue	Fixed assets
Gross profit	Current liabilities
Net sales	Net worth
Rent	Bank
Electricity	Creditors
Cost of sales	Retained profit

Q20: Potential **shareholders** are interested in a public limited companies financial accounts to see if the return on investment will be high enough. They can find this information on the Internet. There are other external users, such as **suppliers**, who will be interested to make sure their goods are paid for on time. Banks will want to make sure that cash **flow** will be sufficient enough to see **overdrafts** being repaid and **creditors** will want to make sure that they are paid promptly for the money they are owed. Only internal users have access to accounts in a **private** limited company. Owners will try and make predications based on past performance. They will look at previous sales **revenue**, gross and net **profit** and expenses. Employees will want to see that their **wages** will be paid, whilst managers will be interested in performance related **bonuses**.

SQA style questions (page 85)

Q21:

- Trading account shows the profit and loss made from buying and selling stock over a period of time.
- Income statement shows the overall profit or loss over a specified time period.
- Statement of financial position which shows the financial position of a business at an exact moment in time.
- Cash budgets show projected income and expenditure for the following year.
- Share prices show the current value of the organisation.

Q22: Any two from:

- Profits need to be calculated accurately.
- Corporation Tax must be accurate.
- PAYE must be calculated for all employees.
- If not PAYE then self-assessed tax returns must be made by employees/duty of organisation to inform about this.

- VAT must be returned regularly.
- Good record keeping.

8 Ratio analysis

Accounting ratios (page 89)

Q1:

	Year 1 fraction	Year 1 %	Year 2 fraction	Year 2 %
Gross % as a % of sales	80000/200000	40	85000/250000	34
Gross profit as a % of cost of goods sold	80000/120000	67	85000/135000	63
Net profit as a % of sales	60000/200000	30	60000/250000	24

Q2: b) False

Q3: a) True

Q4: b) False

Q5: a) True

Q6: b) False

Q7: a) True

Q8: a) True

Q9: b) False

Q10: b) False

Q11: b) False

Current and acid test ratios (page 92)

Q12:

Ratio	Alpha Ltd	Beta Ltd
Current ratio	45000 : 30000 = 1.5 :1	46000 : 23000 = 2 : 1
Acid Test ratio	(45000 - 16000) : 30000 = 0.96 : 1	(46000 - 20000) : 23000 = 1.13 : 1

Answers from page 93.

Q13:

	2014	2015
Sainsbarn plc	533/4751 × 100 = **11.22**%	625/4848 ×100 = **12.89**%
Spender plc	440.5/4565.8 × 100 = **9.64**%	643.8/3080.9 ×100 = **20.90**%
Morris's plc	204.3/993.1 ×100 = **20.57**%	229.8/1113.7 = **20.63**%

Mearns plc ratios (page 94)

Q14:

	20x1 ratio	20x1	20x2 ratio	20x2
Gross % as a % of sales	70/250	28%	110/320	34.37%
Gross profit as a % of cost of goods sold	70/180	38.88%	110/210	52.38%
Net profit as a % of sales	50/250	20%	70/320	21.87%
Current ratio	105 : 55	1.9 : 1	128 : 68	1.88 : 1
Acid test ratio	(105 - 30) : 55	1.36 : 1	(128 - 40) : 68	1.29 : 1
Return on capital employed	50/150	30%	70/150	46.66%

Summary questions (page 95)

Q15: b) False

Q16: b) False

Q17: a) True

Q18: a) True

Q19: a) True

Q20: b) False

Q21: b) False

Q22: a) True

Q23: a) True

Q24: b) False

End of topic 8 test (page 96)

Q25: a; c

Q26: b; d

Q27: a; d

Q28: b; c; d

Q29: a

SQA style questions (page 97)

Q30: Any four from:

- **Current ratio:** Current assets/current liabilities - shows the ability to pay short term debts, 2:1 is the accepted ratio.

- **Acid test ratio:** Current assets - stock/current liabilities - shows the ability to pay short term debts quickly, 1:1 is the accepted ratio.

- **Gross profit ratio:** Gross profit/sales x 100 - measures the percentage profit made from buying and selling stock.

- **Net profit ratio:** Net profit/sales x 100 - measures the percentage profit after expenses have been paid.

- **Return on Capital Employed:** Net profit/opening capital x 100 - measures the return on capital for investors in a business, can be compared to other organisations or a safe investment such as a building society.

- **Mark Up:** Gross profit/cost of goods sold x 100 - measures how much is added to the cost of goods for profit.

Q31:

- Information is historical, which means it might not be as useful today.

- Does not take into account external factors, which means a period of recession may skew the results.

- Does not show the staff morale, which means a business may be performing as well as the figures suggest.

- Does not take into account recent investments, which means decisions may be taken on outdated information.

- Can only compare similar organisations with similar size and market, which means not all results will be accurate.

9 Technology

Use of technology - revision (page 100)

Q1:   1c; 2f; 3k; 4b; 5h; 6a; 7l; 8g; 9e; 10i; 11d; 12j

Brown Manufacturing Ltd (page 105)

Expected answer

Cash budget of Brown Manufacturing Ltd

	January £	February £	March £	April £	May £
Opening balance	25,000	45,500	56,000	79,300	43,300
Cash in					
Sales	55,000	49,000	59,000	46,000	60,000
Total cash in	55,000	49,000	59,000	46,000	60,000
Cash out					
Purchases	22,000	26,000	23,000	30,000	24,000
Wages	4,800	4,600	5,000	44,000	5,100
Warehouse	1,200	1,400	1,200	1,500	1,200
Marketing	1,500	1,500	1,500	1,500	1,500
Administration expenses	1200	1200	1200	1200	1200
Distribution expenses	3000	3000	3000	3000	3000
Power	800	800	800	800	800
Total cash out	34,500	38,500	35,700	82,000	36,800
Closing balance	45,500	56,000	79,300	43,300	66,500

Costs and benefits of using ICT (page 108)

Q2:   Employees working from home require access to **email** to allow them to communicate with team mates, suppliers and customers. Meetings can take place from employees home with the use of **video conferencing**. Using a PC/laptop and a **webcam**, video conferencing software allows people to conduct face-to-face meetings using audio and video feeds. ICT is used extensively during the recruitment and selection process. **Word processing** software is used to draw up Job Descriptions and Person Specifications. A business can chose to post vacancies to their own website or use a dedicated recruitment **website**. Once appointed, a business will want to train its workforce. Online training using the **internet** give businesses more flexibility. They are expensive to create, but can be accessed via training providers. Budgets and financial statements are often produced using accounting software or a **spreadsheet** package. This means that changes can be made to the budget very easily. Businesses can use **databases** to store data securely. This software allows them to sort and filter the data.

Summary questions (page 109)

Q3: a) True

Q4: a) True

Q5: b) False

Q6: b) False

Q7: b) False

Q8: a) True

Q9: a) True

Q10: b) False

End of topic 9 test (page 110)

Q11: 1c; 2a; 3e; 4f; 5b; 6g; 7d

Q12: Initial and on-going costs of **hardware** and equipment can be expensive for business. They also must deal with the on-going costs of replacing and **upgrading** systems. Staff also need to be trained to ensure they are **competent** in using the machinery. This can lead to a loss of working time. ICT programs may be susceptible to computer viruses or **hackers**, which are people who intentionally try and steal or corrupt your data. Staff may also feel the impact of continually working at a computer, with symptoms such as repetitive **strain** injury, backache or eyestrain. A business can use ICT to complete tasks more quickly, which leads to increased **efficiency**. Edits can also be made, leading to greater **flexibility**. Sending out standardised information leads to increased customer **satisfaction**. Streamlining processes can also lead to a **competitive** edge until rivals catch up.

SQA style questions (page 110)

Q13: Any three from:

- ICT increases productivity due to the use of machinery which can allow for more products to be made.
- It reduces waste as technology makes fewer mistakes and this increases profit.
- A consistent quality of product is made which can increase customer satisfaction.
- It can mean that less staff are needed which reduces overall staffing costs/increases profits.
- It improves the speed of communication due to the use of e-mail or intranets which makes decision making quicker.

- It increases the access to information which should result in a more informed, better decision being made.

- Technology can be used in situations that are hazardous to workers which results in less accidents to the workforce.

- Accuracy should be increased as technology results in less mistakes especially when carrying out large calculations resulting in improved customer satisfaction.

Q14: Any three from:

- Use of e-mail which will speed up sending training files to colleagues throughout the world. Attachments can be inserted for colleagues to view.

- Use of videoconferencing will allow disciplinary meetings to take place without travelling meaning travel costs can be reduced.

- Increased access to information through the use of the internet and access to worldwide sources will allow organisations to look at new legislation.

- File sharing of training programmes can be carried out anywhere in the world through the organisations network which will improve decision making as files can be shared and worked on at same time by colleagues anywhere in the world.

- It saves on costs as training can take place online.

- It saves on labour costs as use of computers will reduce labour requirements.

- It allows for more flexible working with staff as they can work from home and stay in contact via ICT allowing for better relationships.

10 End of unit tests

End of unit 3 test (page 112)

Q1: a) Selection

Q2: b) Recruitment

Q3: b) Recruitment

Q4: a) Selection

Q5: a) True

Q6: b) Flase

Q7: b) Flase

Q8: a) True

Q9: a) True

Q10: c) Venture capitalists

Q11: a) Bank loan

Q12: b) Commercial mortgage

Q13: 1b; 2a; 3c

Q14: Work-based training course are developed and led by staff within an organisation. They can include a mixture of on-the-job and off-the-job initiatives.

Q15: Off-the-job training takes place when an employee is not doing the job. This can involve a workshop with an in-house trainer or attending an external training course.

Q16: On-the-job training takes place whilst the employees is doing their job. This can involve being coached by a more experienced colleague.

Q17: Induction training is used for new staff and includes information such as the organisations layout and health and safety requirements.

Q18: Virtual training involves making use of online resources and discussion forums to up-skill or explore ideas with colleagues and other professionals.

Q19: 1f; 2c; 3a; 4d; 5b; 6e

Q20: a) True

Q21: b) False

Q22: b) False

Q23: a) True

SQA style questions (page 115)

Q24: Any five from:

- Local newspapers are relatively inexpensive to advertise in and will attract applicants who are able to travel to work.

- National newspapers are more expensive with the benefit of having a higher readership; the pool of applicants is much wider but many may feel unable to apply because of geography.

- Recruitment agencies could be used - these are expensive as they charge a fee but the benefit is they have contact details for a number of prospective employees and will email them regularly with possible vacancies that match their skills.

- Local schools/colleges can be contacted to advertise vacancies to leavers.

- HR managers are increasingly using job vacancy websites such as s1jobs.com; the searching by job or by area feature of these websites makes it easy for prospective employees to find current vacancies; the downside to these sites is the fact they are online and open to anyone - a business may be inundated with applicants, not all of whom may be suitable.

- Large organisations can use their own website to feature current vacancies - this will be cheaper than using a third party website but is unlikely to have the same number of people accessing the site.

Q25: Any eight from:

- **Costs**
  - Financial costs of external courses must be considered.
  - Working time is lost if the employee is away from the business for a period of time.
  - Quality of work may be poorer/slower when staff are training.
  - Resistance to the benefits of training - employees need to understand why the training is being delivered.

- **Benefits**
  - Increased staff motivation as they can see that the business is contributing to their personal development.
  - Improves flexibility of staff as they can work across different departments.
  - Increased production levels as staff are more capable.
  - Increased competence of staff and staff are more highly skilled.
  - Easier for employers to introduce change.
  - Image of business improves as less mistakes are made.

(Maximum of 4 marks available if only costs or only benefits are mentioned.)

Q26: Any six from:

- **Autocratic advantages**
  - Tasks are clearly defined.
  - Quick decision making.
  - Few opportunities for staff to make mistakes unnoticed by management.

- ○ Suitable for boring, repetitive jobs with no intrinsic motivation.
- ○ Works well in an urgent situation where immediate action is needed and there is no time for discussion.
- ○ Ensures that decisions are taken by those most experienced i.e. managers.
- **Autocratic disadvantages**
  - ○ Subordinates' creativity is not used.
  - ○ Supervision is expensive in terms of management time.
  - ○ Lack of freedom to make decisions is demotivating for subordinates.
  - ○ Subordinates are not given the opportunity to prepare for promotion.
- **Democratic advantages**
  - ○ Uses employees' imagination and knowledge which results in more ideas.
  - ○ Motivates employees by involving them in decisions.
  - ○ Prepares subordinates for promotion by giving them more responsibility.
- **Democratic disadvantages**
  - ○ Involving more people will make the decision-making process more time-consuming.
  - ○ Some employees gain a feeling of security from being supervised closely.
  - ○ Some employees may believe it is the manager's job to make decisions and resent being expected to come up with ideas.
  - ○ Objectives may be forgotten if people's needs become the manager's primary focus.

Q27: Any four from:

- Positive employee relations allow staff to feel empowered when employees are given the power to make certain decisions without consulting the manager each time.
- Positive employee relations use appraisals - when staff meet with a line manager to discuss their progress and set targets for the future, the result of this is often increased productivity.
- Positive employee relations increase the opportunities for promotion.
- Trade union/professional association recognition reduces the risk of strike action which benefits both management and the workforce.
- Positive employee relations can be used as a great PR exercise for the organisation.

Q28: Any two of the following legislations. You should give two points for each legislation mentioned.

- **Employment Rights Act 1996**
  States the duties and rights of the employer and employee and includes:
  - ○ the employee's rights to maternity and paternity leave;
  - ○ termination of employment;
  - ○ the right to a written contract of employment within 60 days of starting work.
- **Working Time Regulations Act 1998**
  - ○ The maximum amount of time an employee can be expected to work;

- o their entitlement to breaks and rest periods;
- o the pattern of work;
- o the length of time you can do night work and their entitlement to leave.
- **Employment Act 2002**
  - o This act gives additional rights for things such as paternity leave, and an extension of some existing rights.
  - o Mothers and fathers of young children under six, or disabled children under 18, have a right to request a flexible working arrangement.
  - o It requires employers to have minimum internal disciplinary and grievance procedures to avoid the need for so many cases to go to industrial tribunals.
- **National Minimum Wage Act 1998**
  - o States the minimum wage that must be paid to employees.
  - o It is set on the recommendations of the Low Pay Commission, an expert panel made up of business figures, trade union leaders and academics.
- **Employment Relations Act 2004**
  - o The operation of the statutory recognition procedure for trade unions;
  - o the law on industrial action ballots and ballot notices;
  - o when arbitration should take place;
  - o unfair dismissal and grievance and disciplinary hearings.

Q29: Any four from:

- Bank Loan - a loan paid back with interest.
- Commercial Mortgage - a loan secured against property owned by the organisation.
- Sell Assets/land - sell unwanted assets to raise funds.
- Venture Capitalists - obtain a loan from a venture capitalist who will receive a share in the organisation in return.
- Retained profits - use retained profits from previous years to fund the takeover.
- Bring in new shareholders with fresh capital.
- Any other appropriate source for a large organisation.

Q30: Any three from:

- Monitors the progress or performance of the organisation which in turn assists with planning and decision making.
- Assesses and demonstrates the validity of a business project and forms part of the information package or business plan presented to a financial lender in order to help secure the required finance.
- As part of a business plan which would be drawn up by a new business prior to starting up; or by an existing business prior to expansion.
- Provides the business with a tool for comparison of budgeted with actual results obtained from other financial statements.

Q31:

- Statement of financial position shows the value of an organisation's assets, the liabilities of the company and the equity of the company at a given point in time - useful when looking at the net worth of a business.

- Income statement shows an organisation's total sales, the cost of production and any profit or loss made over the period of one year - useful when looking at the profitability of a business.

Q32: Any four from:

- **Current ratio:** current assets/current liabilities shows the ability to pay short term debts, answer of 2:1 is the accepted ratio.

- **Acid test ratio:** current assets - stock/current liabilities shows the ability to pay short term debts quickly, 1:1 is the accepted ratio.

- **Gross profit ratio:** gross profit/sales x 100 measures the percentage profit made from buying and selling stock.

- **Net profit ratio:** net profit/sales x 100 measures the percentage profit after expenses have been paid.

- **Return on capital employed:** net profit/opening capital x 100 measures the return on capital for investors in a business, can be compared to other organisations or a safe investment such as a building society.

- **Mark Up:** gross profit/cost of good sold x 100 measures how much is added to the cost of goods for profit.

Q33: Any four from:

- Formulae can be used to calculate information.
  - Allows for automatic calculation if anything changes.
  - Reduces error.
- Information can be saved and edited later.
- Templates can be used for financial information - e.g. Cash Budgets/Profit Statements.
- Standardisation of documents means that processes are easily replicated.
- Graphs/charts can be created to display information.
  - Allows easier comparison of difficult financial information.